Krafty Kiddos

Milestones

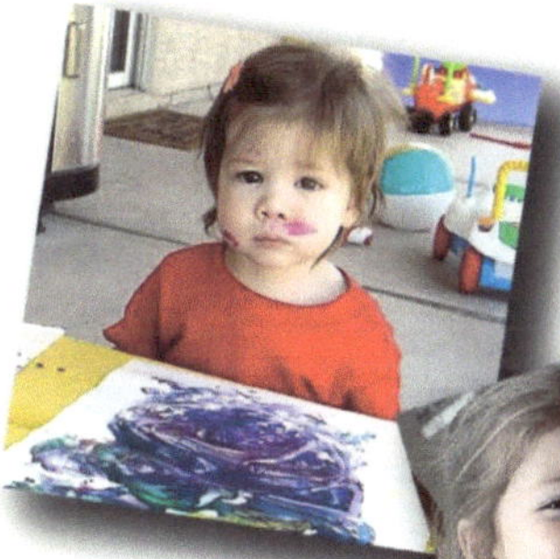

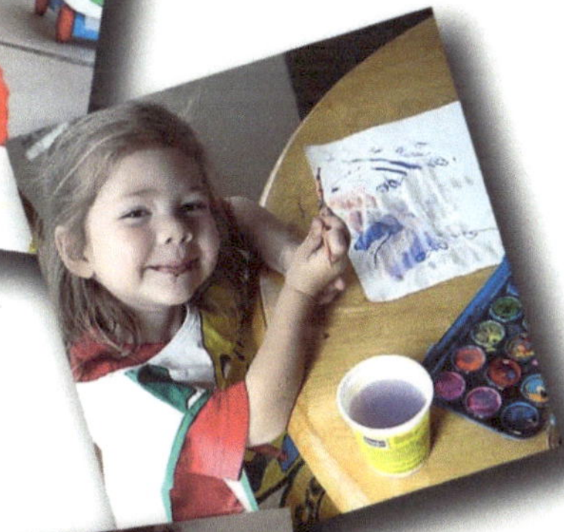

Art Activities
For Kiddos
Ages 1-12

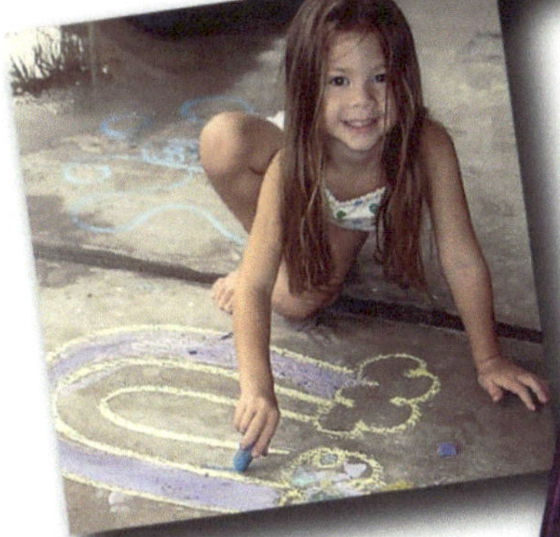

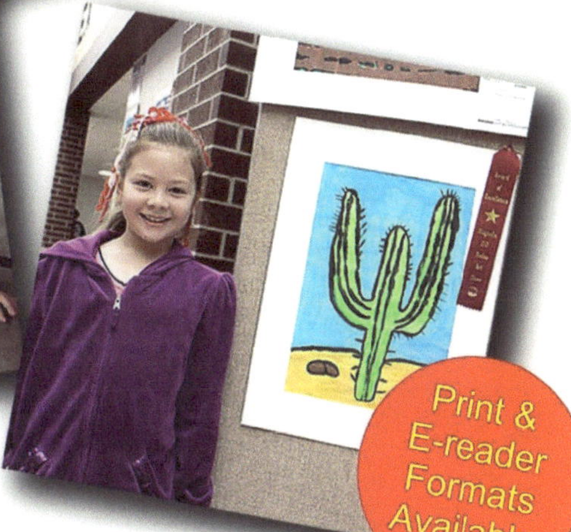

Print &
E-reader
Formats
Available

Written & Illustrated by
Victoria Satory

Limit of Liability & Disclaimer of Warranty

The author makes no representations or warranties with respect to the accuracy or completeness of the contents of this work and specifically disclaims all warranties, including without limitation warranties of fitness for a particular purpose. No warranty may be created or extended by sales or promotional materials. The advice and strategies contained herein may not be suitable for every individual or situation. This work is sold with the understanding that the author is not engaged in rendering legal, technical, or other professional services. If professional assistance is required, the services of a competent professional person should be sought. The author shall not be liable for damages arising here from. The fact that an organization or website is referred to in this work as a citation and/or a potential source of further information does not mean that the author endorses the information that the organization or website may provide or the recommendations it may make. Further, readers should be aware that websites listed in this work may have changed or disappeared between when this work was written and when it is read.

Format & Permission

This book is available in print and electronic format. Content and presentation may differ between formats. No part of this publication may be reproduced, stored in a retrieval system, or transmitted in any form or by any means, electronic, mechanical, photocopying, recording, scanning, or otherwise, without the prior written permission of the author. Requests should be addressed to Victoria Satory at permission@kraftykiddos.com.

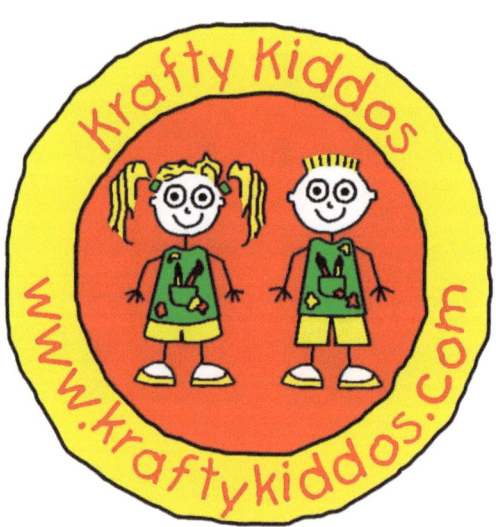

© 2015 Victoria Satory

One Year

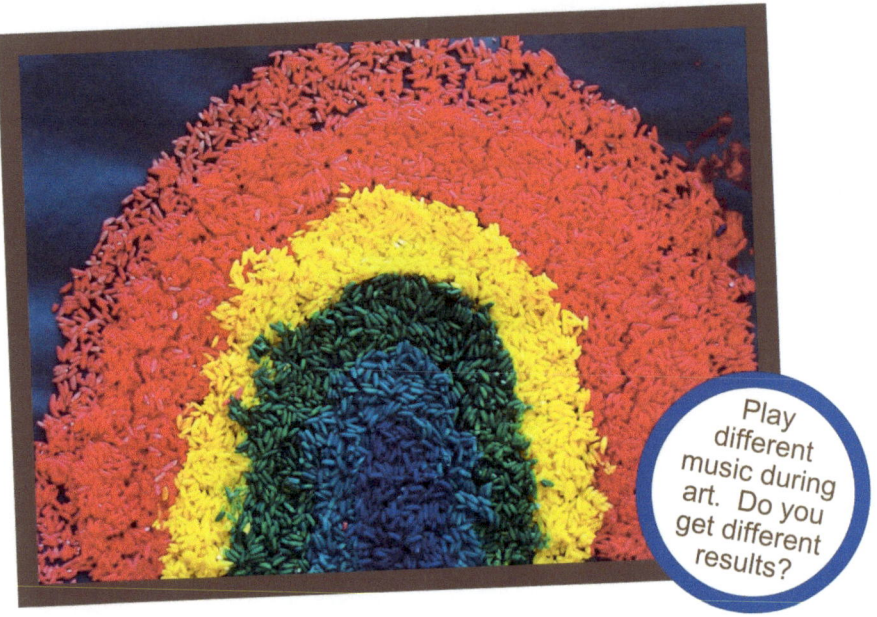

Play different music during art. Do you get different results?

One year olds actively explore the world around them. They like to touch, shake, and throw things! They are either walking or on the verge of walking and they often imitate gestures. They understand simple commands and giggle at games like "Peek-a-boo", "Pat-a-cake", and "Piggies". They will hand you a book if they want to hear a story. They respond emotionally to music and enjoy viewing pictures of familiar people and objects.

Bright colors and high contrast patterns capture their attention. One year olds have limited hand dexterity, but can still typically grab things using their thumb and pointer finger. They enjoy putting items in containers, dumping them out, and putting them in again.

Activities

Finger Paint

Try pudding, shaving cream, or dry milk instead of paint and feet instead of hands! Stick with primary colors to avoid everything turning brown.

Textures

Place textured items in a box to explore. Include items such as sand paper, feathers, carpet, wood, hair brushes, combs, etc.

Sorting

Teach colors and improve dexterity by sorting items such as colored cereals bowl to bowl. Avoid items that could be a choking hazard.

Tissues

Pull tissues from the box one by one then replace them with colored tissue paper. Count aloud as they are pulled to learn both numbers and colors.

Coloring

Color with oversized crayons or sidewalk chalk. For easy cleanup, try Color Wonder art supplies that only work on special Color Wonder paper.

OVERPAINT

Paint construction paper, a canvas, or even newspaper again and again. The colors will darken with each layer and you will save on paper!

Mirroring

Paint one half of a piece of paper then fold the sides together. Unfold the paper to see the same image on both sides.

Shake Paint

Place rice or some other substance in a zipper bag with a spoonful of paint. Shake the bag, remove the colored rice, and repeat with a new color.

SANDPRINTS

Step 1   Put a layer of sand in a pie tin

Step 2   Wet the sand

Step 3   Place foot or hand in sand and push

Step 4   Mix plaster and pour into sand imprint

Step 5   Insert paperclip into plaster for hanging

Step 6   Let dry, remove, and hang

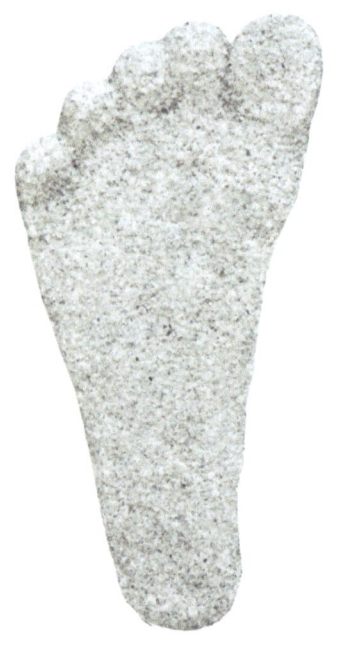 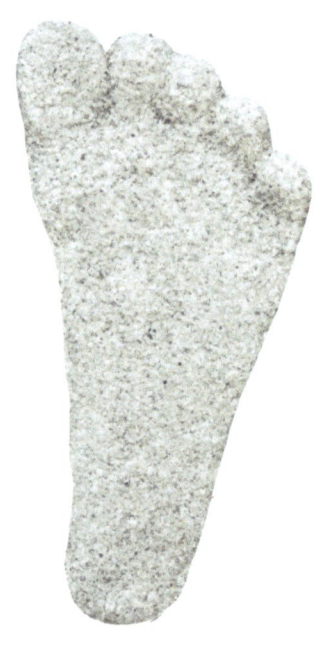

Make extras in case some of them break and consider using colored sand. Footprints are typically easier to make than handprints.

Contact Paper

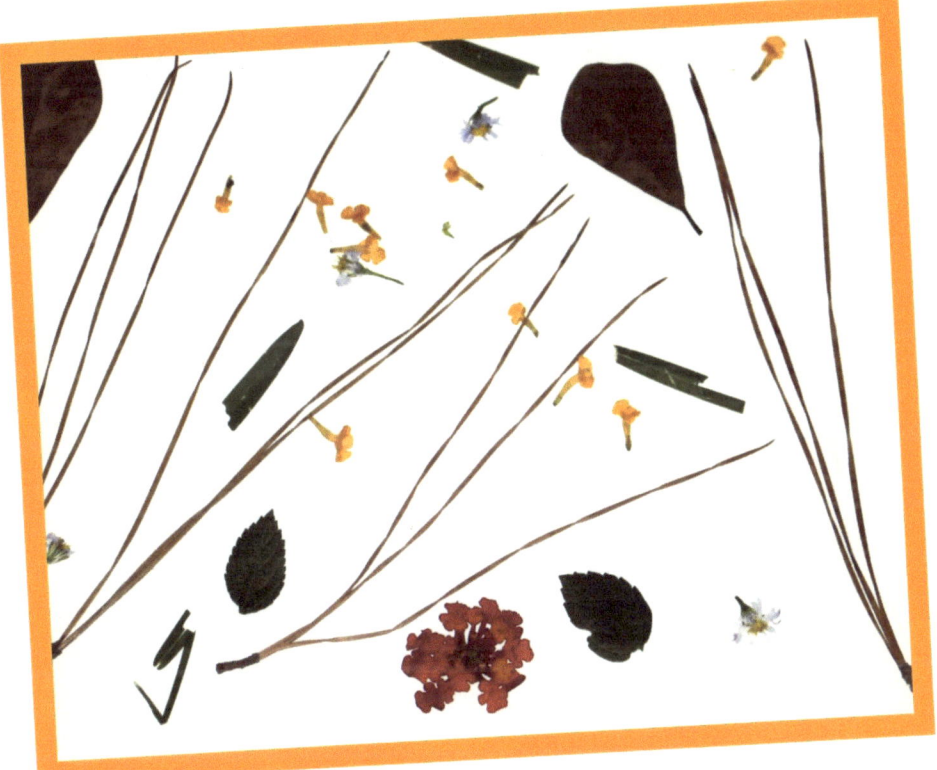

Use tissue paper instead of leaves and two pieces of contact paper to create sun catchers.

Step 1   Lie down a piece of clear contact paper

Step 2   Find leaves, grass, flowers, etc.

Step 3   Place the items on the contact paper

Step 4   Put a piece of paper on top

Step 5   Turn the picture over and enjoy

Scribbles

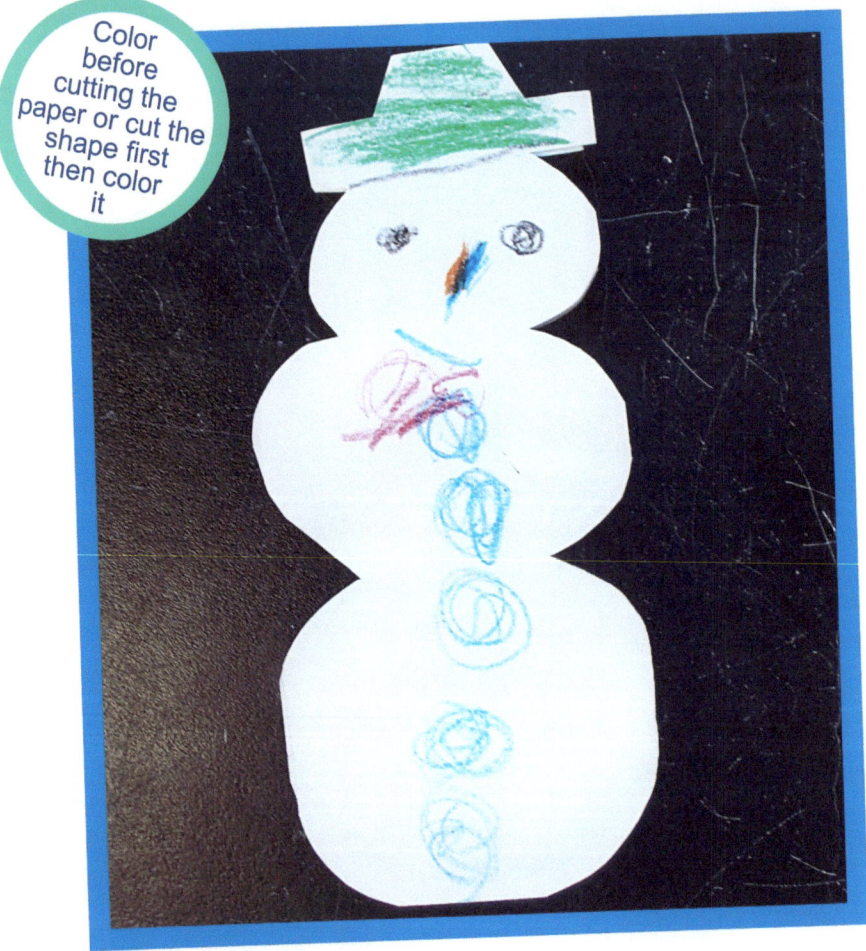

Color before cutting the paper or cut the shape first then color it

Save those scribbles! Cut recognizable shapes out of toddlers' coloring.
Make hearts, flowers, animals, snowflakes, trucks, houses, and more.

Step 1   Cut a recognizable shape from paper

Step 2   Color the shape

Step 3   Add any extras like glitter, buttons, etc.

Santa's Reindeer

Step 1   Paint foot and hands with fabric paint

Step 2   Place prints on shirt

Step 3   Apply eyes and nose using fabric glue

Step 4   Decorate shirt with crayons or markers

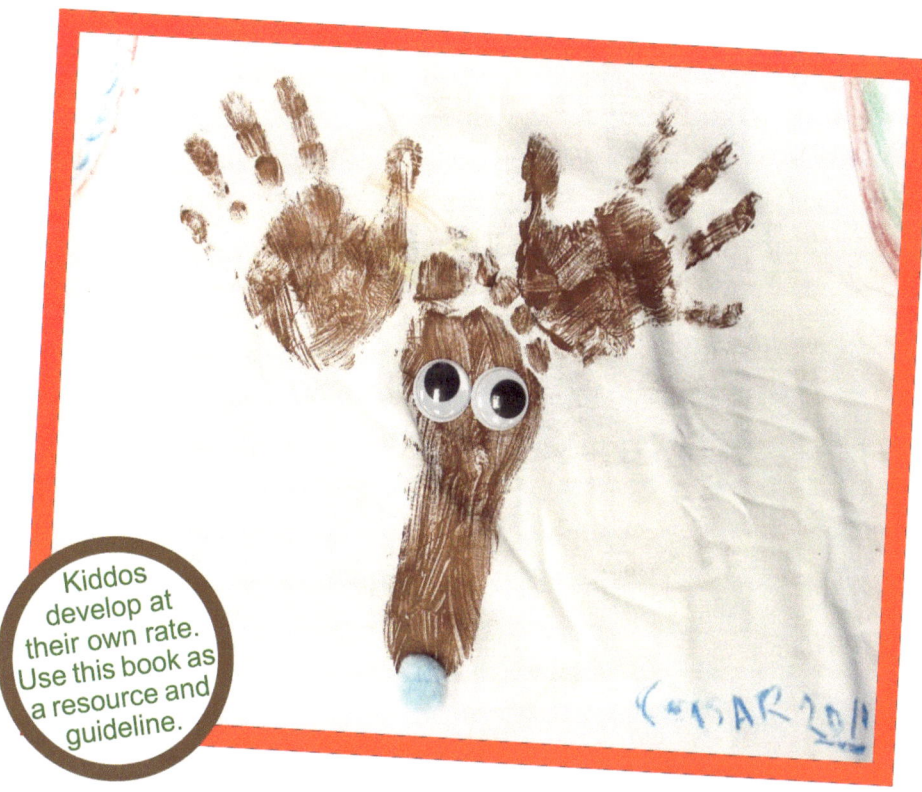

Kiddos develop at their own rate. Use this book as a resource and guideline.

Make handprint shirts of all different animals!

TwO YeaRs

Two year olds have their own likes and dislikes and enjoy making their own decisions. With weak communication skills and poor emotional control, outbursts are common. They enjoy the same books again and again, often memorizing the words. They like puzzles, can name at least six body parts, and recognize opposites. They talk about themselves and are very curious. They enjoy being around other children though they mainly play "beside" them rather than "with" them. They can follow simple two part directions and may favor one hand over the other.

Two year olds typically have a favorite art activity and enjoy the process, caring little about the outcome. They can build towers of around six blocks, sort by shape or color, and draw straight lines and circles. They have short attention spans, so art stations are very effective.

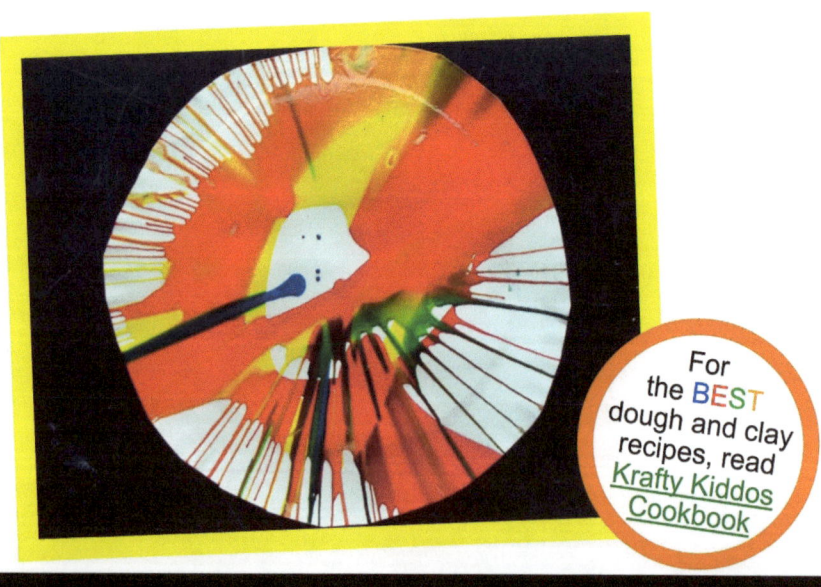

For the BEST dough and clay recipes, read Krafty Kiddos Cookbook

Activities

Brush Paint

If painting is taking too long, try a larger brush and if it's going too fast, use a smaller one! Learn to rinse brushes between colors and use paint sparingly.

Sponge Paint

Use different shaped sponges to make pictures. You can even try cutting your own! It's a fun way to learn letters, numbers, and shapes.

Stamping

Stamp on paper or even clay. Make cards, pictures, and more. Buy self-inking stamps or try making your own stamps using foam stickers!

Spin Art

Drip paint onto a piece of paper inside a salad spinner to make beautiful abstract pictures. Try using different colors and types of paint.

Dot Paint

Brush handles, cotton swabs, and bingo markers work well for making dots of paint and ink. Try making an entire picture out of only dots.

Play Dough

Buy or make your own dough, but use only one color at a time to avoid mixing colors. If it falls onto carpet, just let it dry then vacuum it up.

TEARING

Toddlers who can't yet cut can simply tear paper instead. Tearing is fun and easy. It's also a good way to use up your scrap paper.

Bubble Wrap

Paint bubble wrap then press it against paper to make interesting designs. Buy extra bubble wrap so there is some for the kids to pop!

ice cream

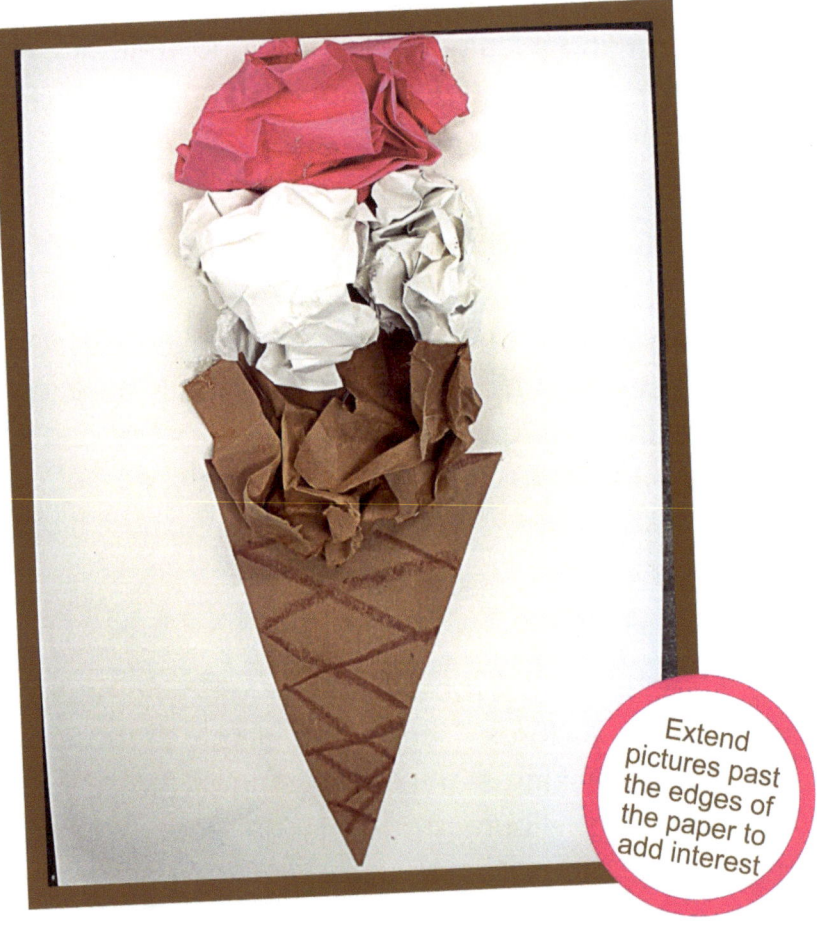

Extend pictures past the edges of the paper to add interest

Make sundaes! Use cotton balls for marshmallow topping or whip cream, pom poms for cherries, yarn for chocolate, and confetti for sprinkles!

Step 1   Crumble paper for the scoops

Step 2   Cut, tear, or draw a cone

Step 3   Glue it all together

Paper Fan

Step 1   Hot glue a popsicle stick to a paper plate

Step 2   Tear paper

Step 3   Glue the paper to the plate

Step 4   Add any extras (eyes, glitter, etc.)

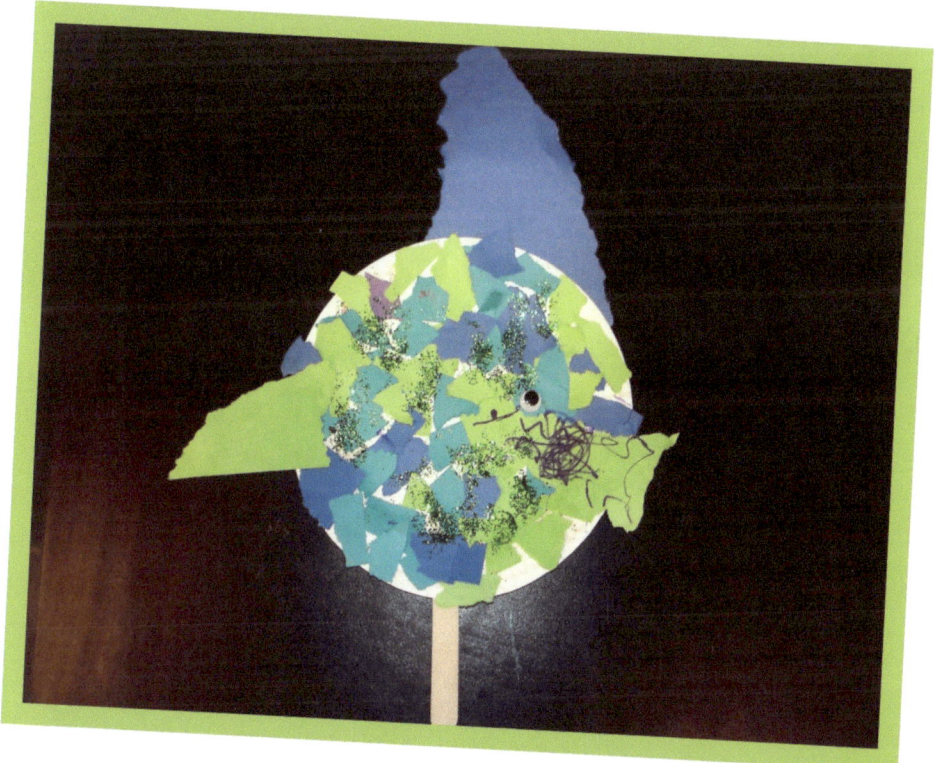

Hot glue the popsicle stick between two paper plates for better stability

Caterpillar

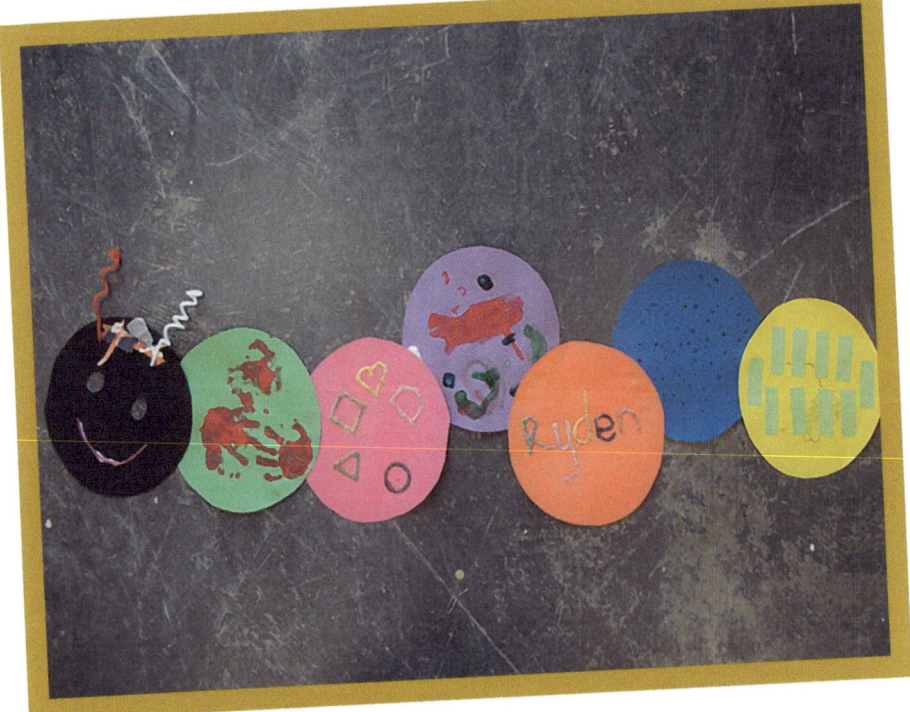

Use different sizes, colors, and shapes for the body. Number or letter the pieces - in multiple languages even! How long will your caterpillar be?

Step 1   Stack several sheets of paper together

Step 2   Trace a circle onto the top sheet

Step 3   Cut around the circle

Step 4   Decorate each piece

Step 5   Glue or brad the circles together

LaDYbUG

Step 1   Cut a paper plate in half (wings)

Step 2   Attach them to a second plate (body)

Step 3   Cut the edge off of a third plate (head)

Step 4   Glue the head to the body

Step 5   Cut antennae from the scraps

Step 6   Glue the antennae to the head

Step 7   Paint and/or decorate the ladybug

Add a stinger to make a bumble bee

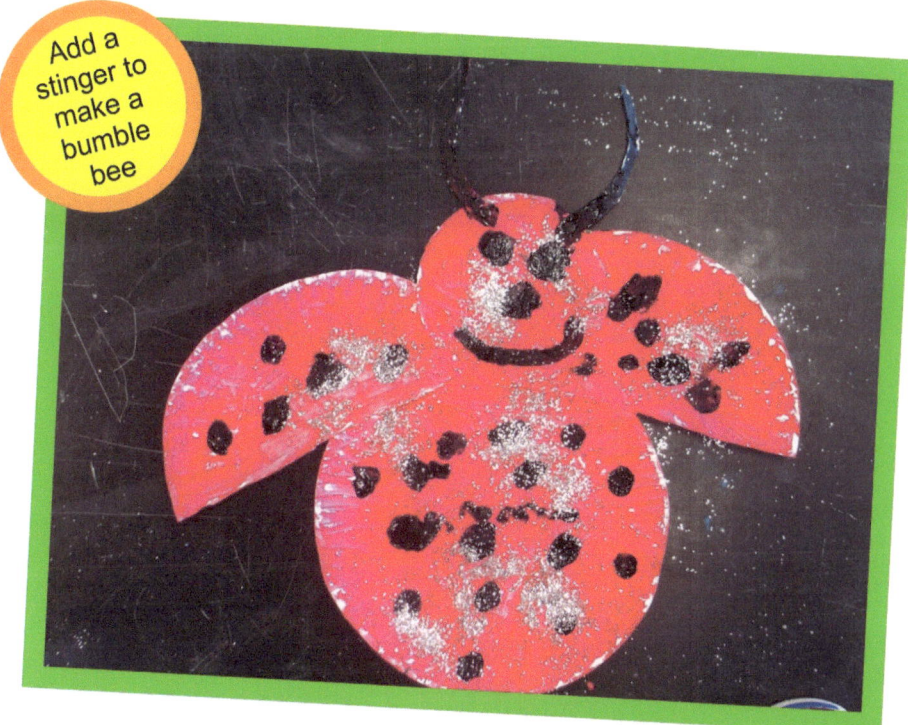

Create movable wings by attaching them with brads

Three Years

Three year olds are growing independent. They have less separation anxiety and enjoy playing with other children. They appreciate routine and have a wider vocabulary for expressing themselves. Gender preferences start to emerge around this age.

Children begin incorporating letters and numbers into their art and they select colors that match their mood. They can now string beads and better understand that for things to stick to paper, glue must first be applied. They attach stories to the pictures they draw and enjoy playing structured games as well as make believe.

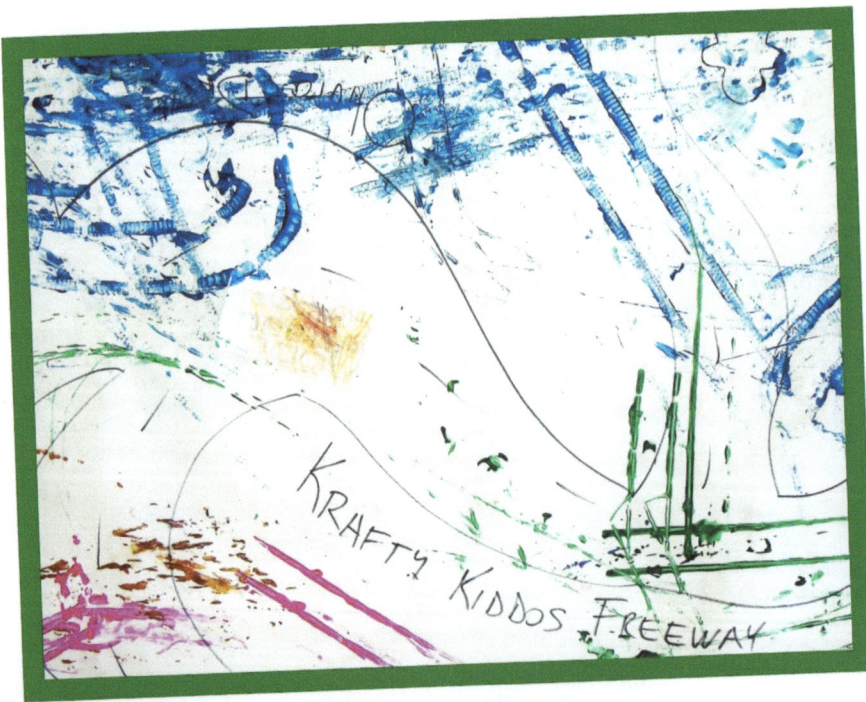

Activities

Paper Squares

Make a bag of cut up paper squares from old scrap paper. Use the paper squares to create pictures and decorate projects.

Beading

Use beads, noodles, or cereal to make necklaces. Slide them over string, yarn, or pipe cleaners. Use different colors to form patterns.

Odds & Ends

Make a bag of odds and ends including yarn, foil, feathers, buttons, ribbon, fabric, etc. Kids can select pieces to glue onto paper or use in projects.

Macaroni Art

Glue different types of noodles onto paper to form pictures perfect for framing. Dye or paint the noodles for added fun.

Cookie Cutters

Dip cookie cutters in paint then press onto paper to create pictures. Use easily recognizable shapes. Smaller cookie cutters work best.

YARN

Drag pieces of yarn through paint or glue and onto paper. Twirl, drip, twist, and flip the yarn around to create colorful abstract art.

Unusual Brushes

Try painting with unusual items like forks, toothbrushes, and combs. This is a wonderful way to learn about texture and explore creativity.

Cars

Run toy cars through paint then drive them across your paper. When you're done, have a tub of soapy water to serve as the car wash!

Fireworks

Step 1   Place paint on a sheet of paper

Step 2   Turn into fireworks using a fork

Step 3   Cut a skyline out of black paper

Step 4   Glue the skyline onto the paper

Step 5   Add glitter to the fireworks

Step 6   Use a cotton swab to add windows

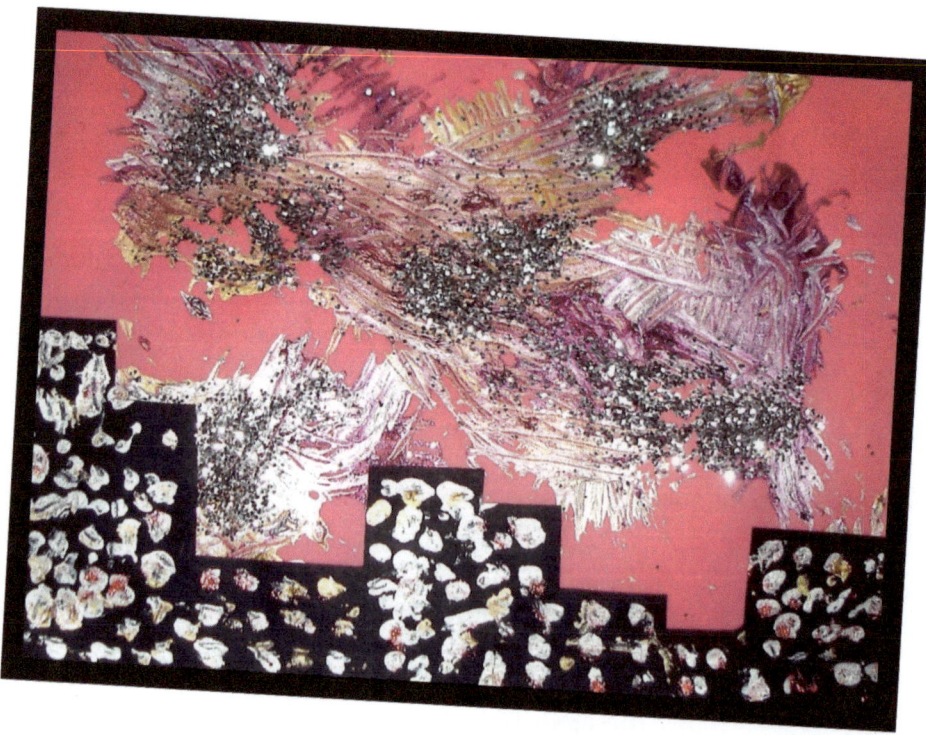

Make skylines of homes, mountains, or national landmarks as well

Masks

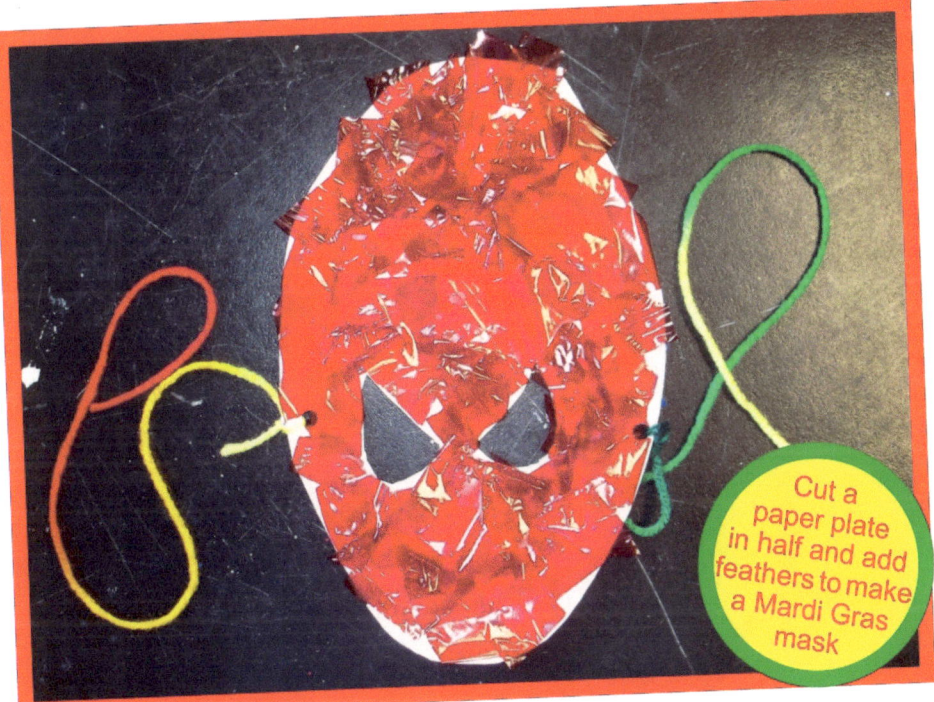

Punch the side holes right by the eye holes for best fit

Cut a paper plate in half and add feathers to make a Mardi Gras mask

Step 1   Cut a paper plate into a shape

Step 2   Cut out eye holes

Step 3   Punch holes in the sides of the plate

Step 4   Paint or decorate the plate

Step 5   Tie yarn to the holes on the sides

Step 6   To use, place on face and tie in the back

Dear Santa

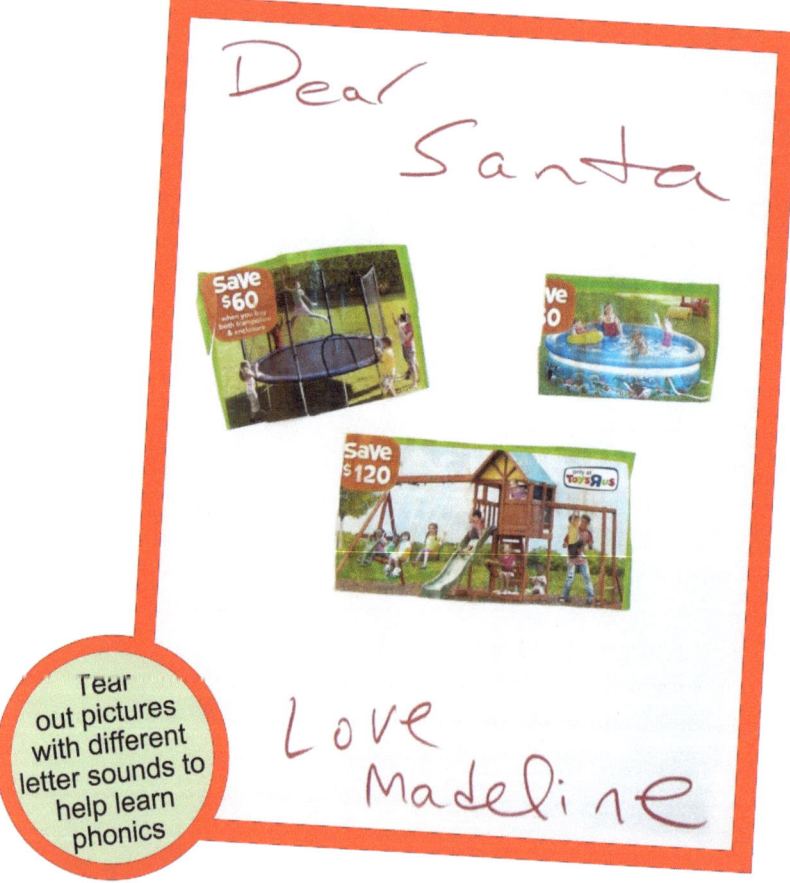

This is a fun and easy way for young children to write letters to Santa

Step 1   Find items you want for Christmas

Step 2   Tear or cut them out

Step 3   Glue the pictures to a piece of paper

Step 4   Write "Dear Santa" at the top

Step 5   Sign your name at the bottom

HANDIMALS

Make a picture using each family member's handprint

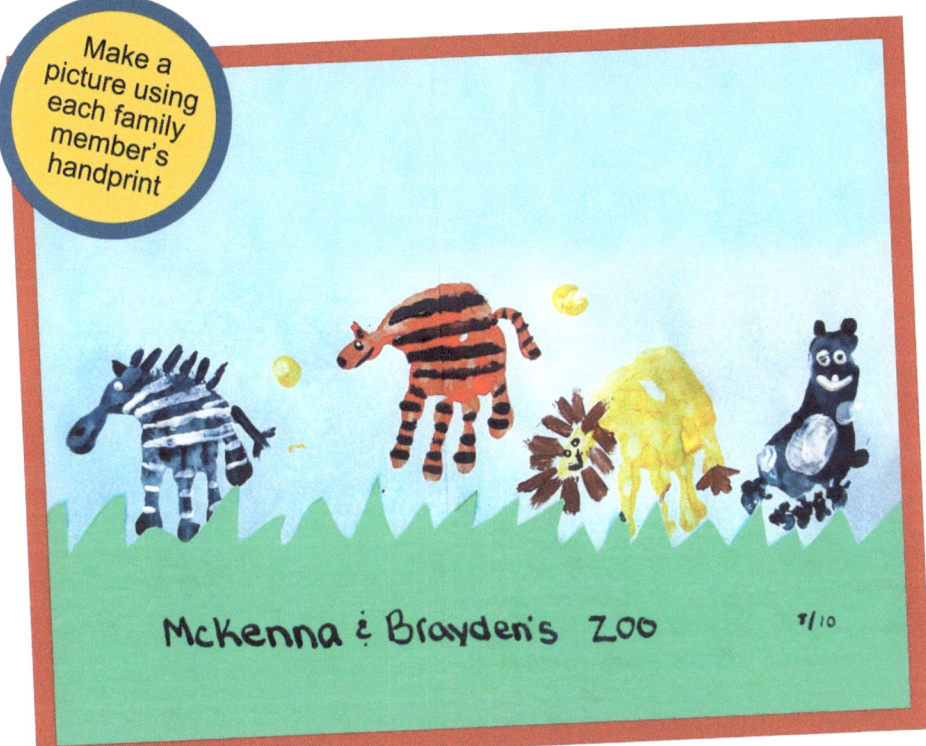

McKenna & Brayden's ZOO   7/10

You don't have to use just hands. Look closely - the bear was made from a footprint!

Step 1   Glue pieces of paper together (optional)

Step 2   Paint your hand

Step 3   Make a handprint on the paper

Step 4   Paint or draw on any detail

Step 5   Cut out grass and glue it to the bottom

Step 6   Sign and date your work of art

FouR Years

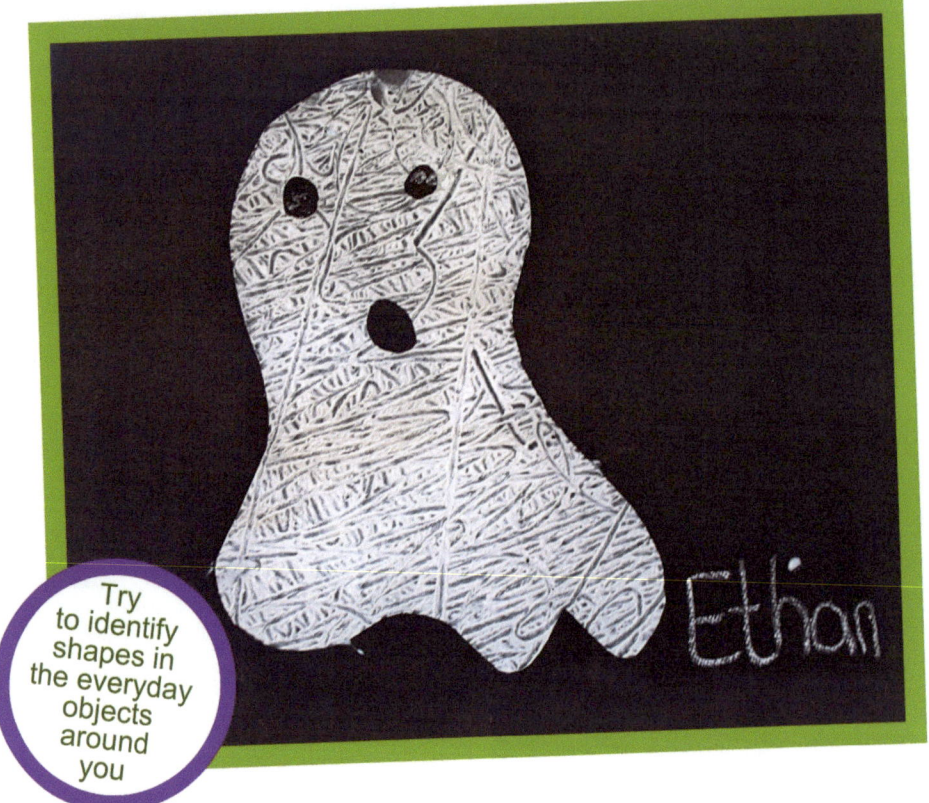

Ethan

Try to identify shapes in the everyday objects around you

Four year olds are very inquisitive and enjoy learning and doing new things. They can follow several instructions at once and enjoy writing their letters and numbers. They know their basic colors and can use scissors. Their pictures are growing more detailed, but are still often incomplete. They can confuse reality and make believe and prefer to play with other children than by themselves. Four year olds use art to reflect their feelings and thoughts.

Activities

Marble Paint

Place paper in a large box lid, drip paint inside (not on the paper), and roll marbles back and forth to make lines across the page.

Sand

Glue colored sand onto paper to make interesting designs or layer colored sand inside bottles and other plastic containers to make decorative pieces.

Bouncy Balls

Place paper and some paint inside a box along with some small rubber balls. Put the lid on and shake! Shoe boxes work well for this.

Paint By Number

Buy a paint by number picture or make your own! For an added challenge, try mixing your own colors from only red, yellow, and blue.

Crayon Resist

Draw a picture in crayon then paint across it with watercolors. The crayon will pop! Try drawing the picture in white crayon on white paper.

PLASTIC WRAP

Paint a picture then place a piece of plastic wrap on top. Rub it around, twirl it, pull straight up, etc. to form different lines and peaks.

Shape Pictures

Cut assorted scrap paper into different shapes and place them in a bag. Select shapes and glue them together to form objects and scenes.

Paint Etching

Use a toothpick or paperclip to scratch lines into wet paint. Write letters or words, draw pictures, or just scratch haphazardly!

Cereal Snail

Step 1   Divide a box of colored cereal by color

Step 2   Place each color in a sandwich bag

Step 3   Roll over each bag with a rolling pin

Step 4   Put glue where the first color should go

Step 5   Pour the crushed cereal over the picture

Step 6   Put the extra cereal back in the bag

Step 7   Repeat procedure for each color used

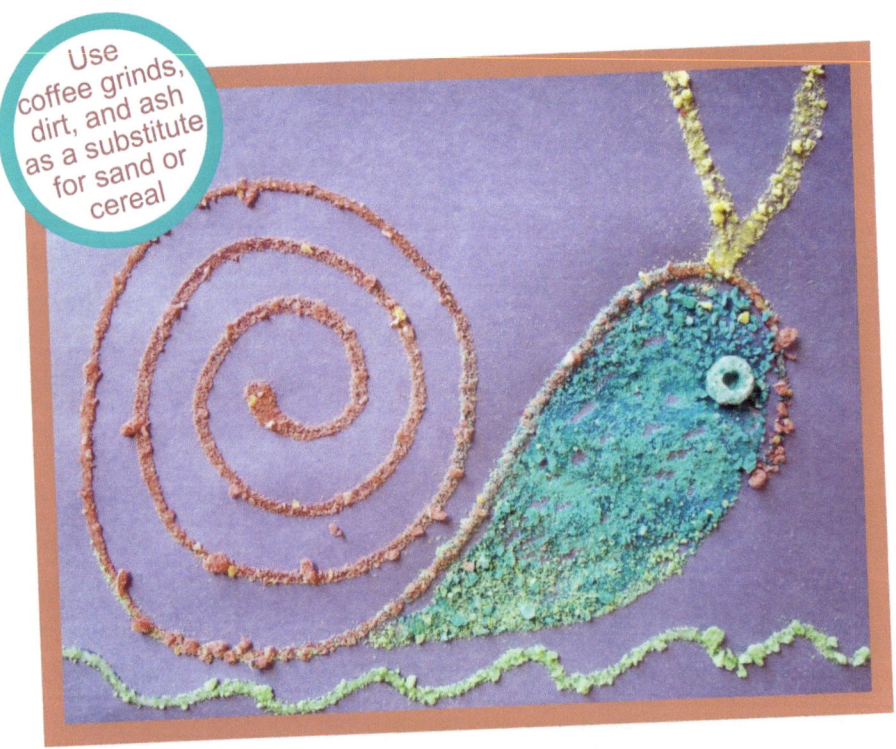

Use coffee grinds, dirt, and ash as a substitute for sand or cereal

Crushed cereal is a fun substitute to using colored sand

U. S. Flag

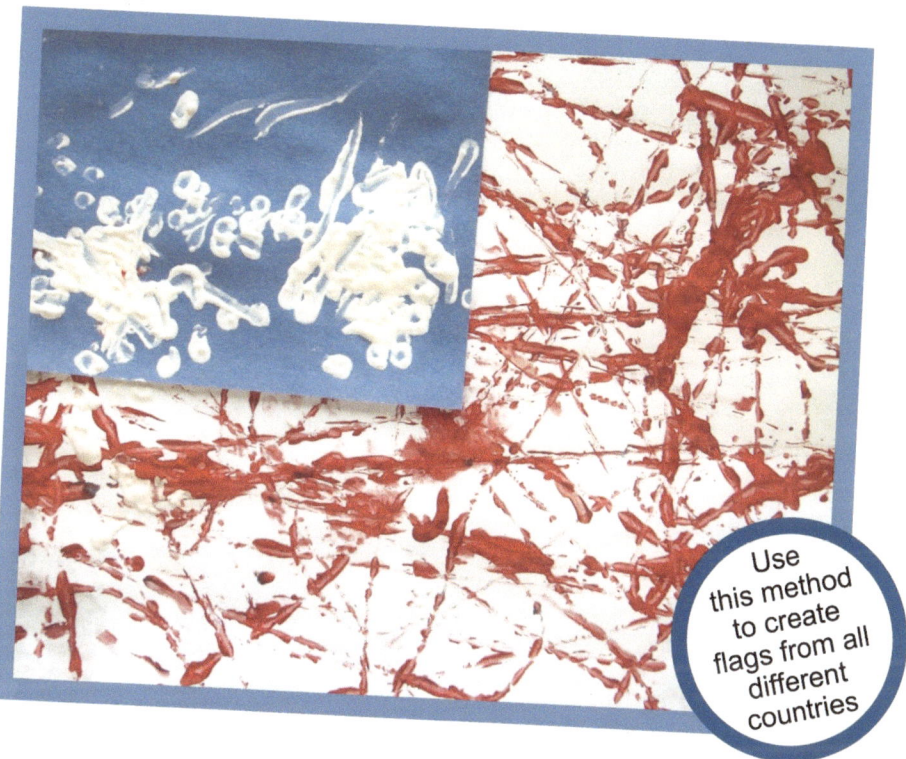

Use this method to create flags from all different countries

Keep track of the marbles because they can be a choking hazard for toddlers

Step 1   Place a sheet of white paper inside a lid

Step 2   Drip red paint on the inside of the lid

Step 3   Roll marbles back and forth in the lid

Step 4   Cut out a square of blue paper

Step 5   Glue the blue paper onto the white paper

Step 6   Dot on stars using a cotton swab

Fish Bowl

Step 1   Cut the top off a paper plate

Step 2   Color the paper plate blue

Step 3   Paint your hand

Step 4   Make a handprint on the plate

Step 5   Glue sand to the bottom of the plate

Step 6   Add a big eye

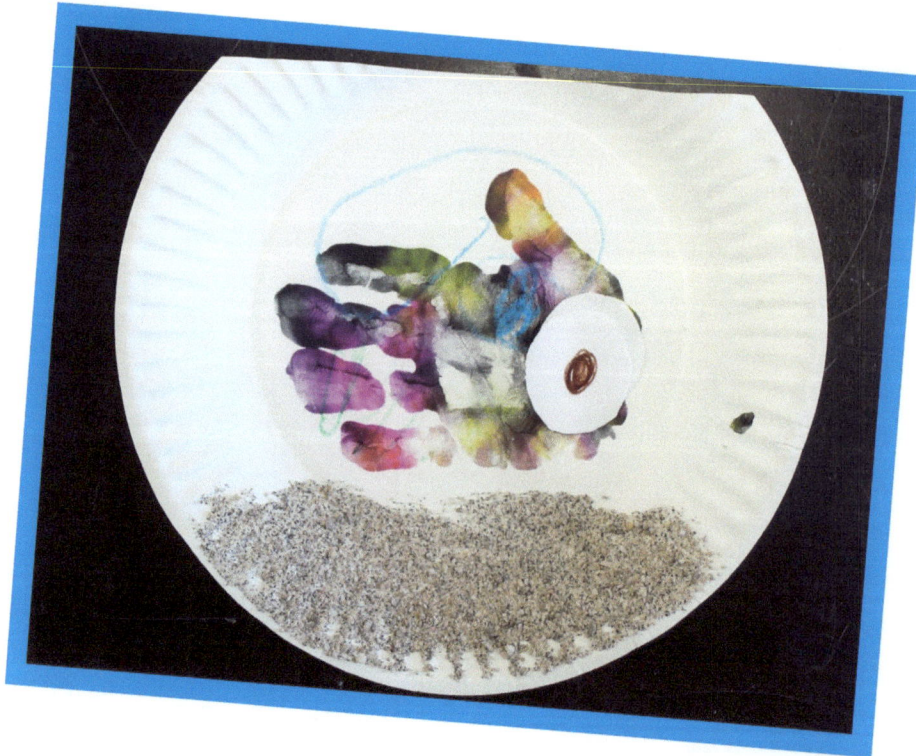

You can also add gravel, tiny shells, green yarn, etc. to your fish bowl

Puppet

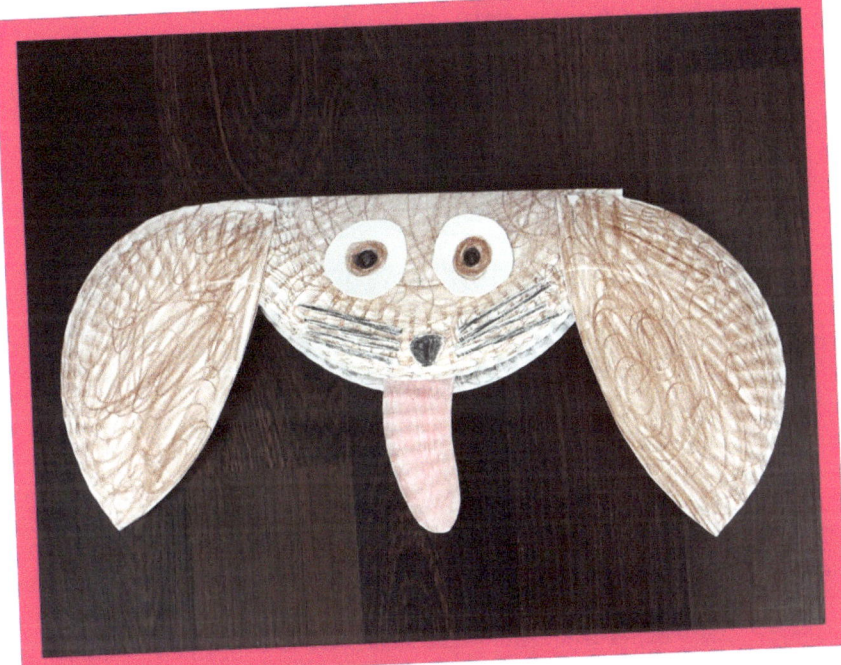

Use a second paper plate or construction paper for the cutouts and attach them using staples, glue, or brads. Paper is preferred because it is lighter.

Step 1   Color the bottom of a paper plate brown

Step 2   Color the top of the plate black

Step 3   Fold the plate in half (black on inside)

Step 4   Cut out eyes, ears, whiskers, etc.

Step 5   Color the cutouts.

Step 6   Attach the cutouts to the plate

Step 7   Press on the plate to make it talk

FiVE YearS

By age five, children are speaking more clearly and in longer sentences. They are learning letter sounds, numbers to 100, and how to write their names. They like to invent games, tell stories, and play with friends.

Their art is becoming more realistic and they can more skillfully paint with either thin or thick brushes. They have a longer attention span and are more likely to follow instruction. They might now include fingers and hair in their drawings of people and commonly use art to tell stories.

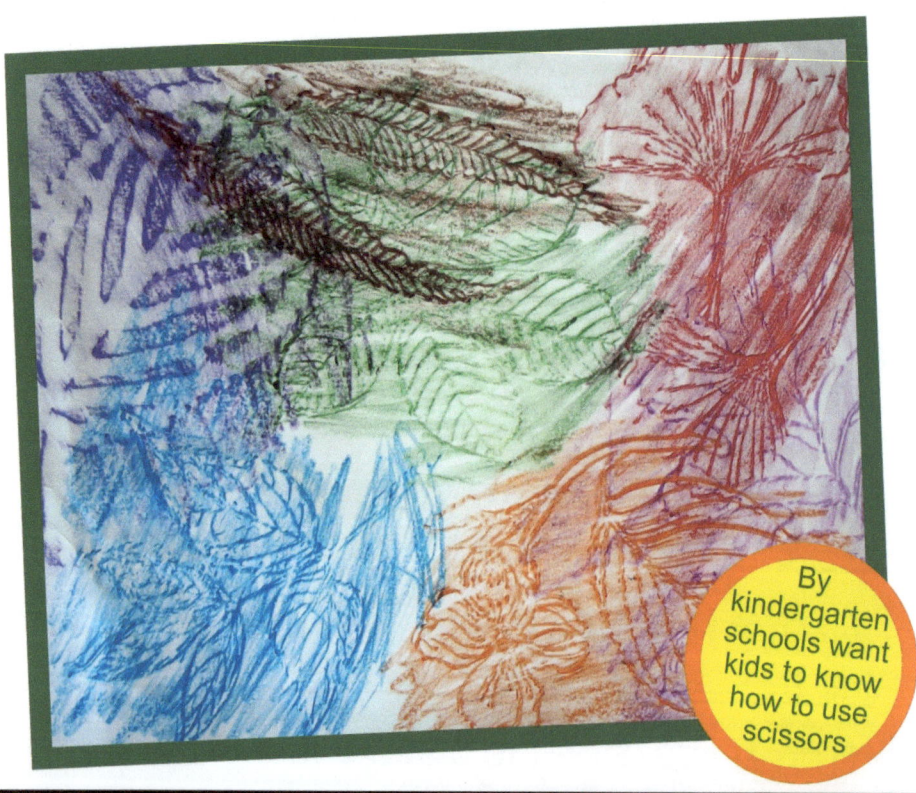

By kindergarten schools want kids to know how to use scissors

Activities

Popsicle Sticks

Glue popsicle sticks together to make picture frames, boxes, boats and more! White glue takes time to dry so use hot glue if you're in a hurry.

Coffee Filters

Color or write on a coffee filter in marker then squirt with water to make the colors spread and mix. The more color you use, the better!

Fingerprints

Make fingerprints on a piece of paper then draw on and around them to turn the prints into different people, animals, and objects.

Mobiles

Popsicle sticks, chopsticks, or hangers can all be used to create mobiles. Color pictures, punch holes, and hang with yarn. Cheap, fun, and easy!

Silly Putty

It bounces, stretches, and even picks up color off some newsprint! Try blue putty, orange, glitter, or even glow in the dark!

INVISIBLE INK

Write on a piece of paper with a cotton swab dipped in lemon juice. Once dry, the writing becomes invisible. Apply heat to reveal the writing.

Rubbings

Place any item with a raised surface, such as a leaf or coin, under a sheet of paper and color. The image will appear on the paper.

Collage

Cut out different pictures from magazines and newspapers then glue them on a sheet of paper, overlapping them with one another.

Fingerprints

Step 1   Press finger onto an ink pad

Step 2   Roll the finger side to side over the paper

Step 3   Draw on and around the prints in ink

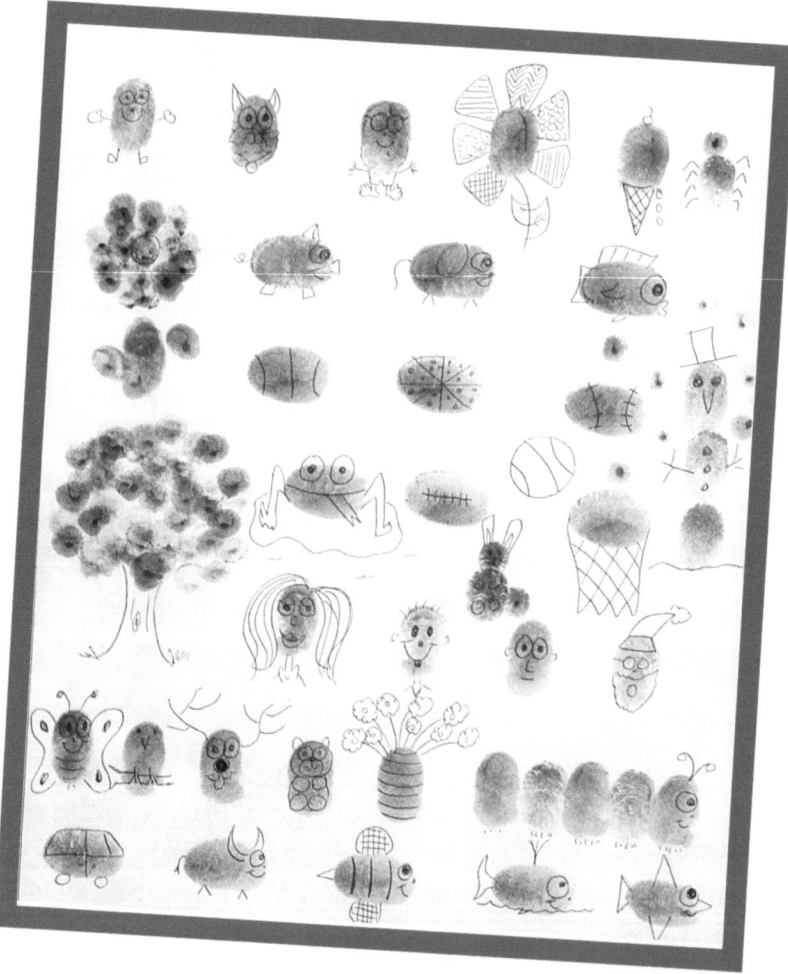

Try using different colored ink and different size fingerprints

Glue & Salt

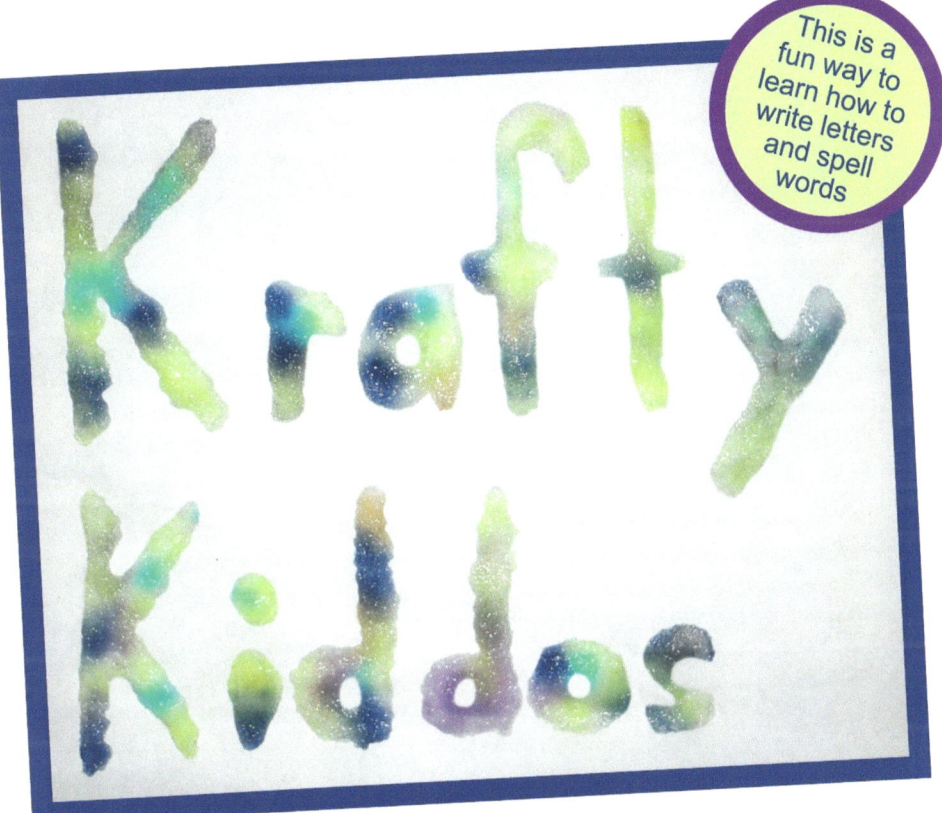

An eye dropper works well for dripping the paint

Step 1   Draw a picture in white glue

Step 2   Pour salt over the lines

Step 3   Shake excess salt from the picture

Step 4   Drip watercolors onto the salt

Picture Frame

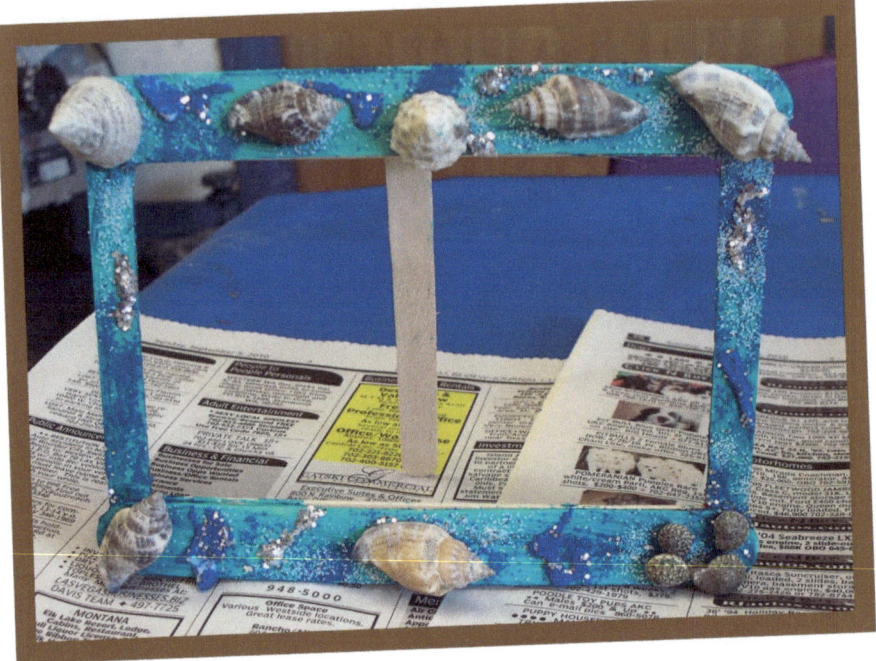

This frame allows you to change out the picture by dropping it in at the top. For a more simple frame, just glue a picture between four craft sticks.

Step 1	Put 2 small sticks on the sides
Step 2	Put 2 large sticks on the top and bottom
Step 3	Glue them all together
Step 4	Glue 2 more small sticks on the sides
Step 5	Glue 1 large stick on the top
Step 6	Glue 1 small stick on the bottom
Step 7	Glue 1 large stick on the bottom
Step 8	Decorate the frame
Step 9	Hot glue 1 small stick as a stand (optional)

PAPER FISH

Step 1   Put two pieces of paper together
Step 2   Cut out a fish shape
Step 3   Staple the edge, leaving a hole
Step 4   Stuff it with newspaper
Step 5   Staple the hole closed
Step 6   Cut or tear squares of paper
Step 7   Glue the paper all over the fish
Step 8   Add the eye
Step 9   Punch a hole in the top to hang

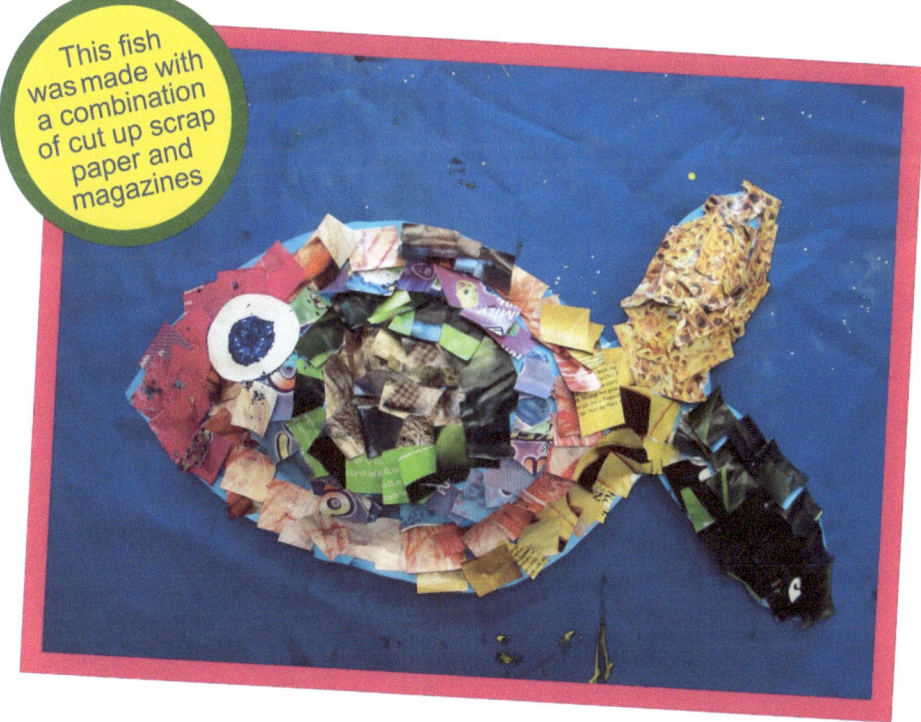

This fish was made with a combination of cut up scrap paper and magazines

Try making other animals and shapes using the same method

Six YearS

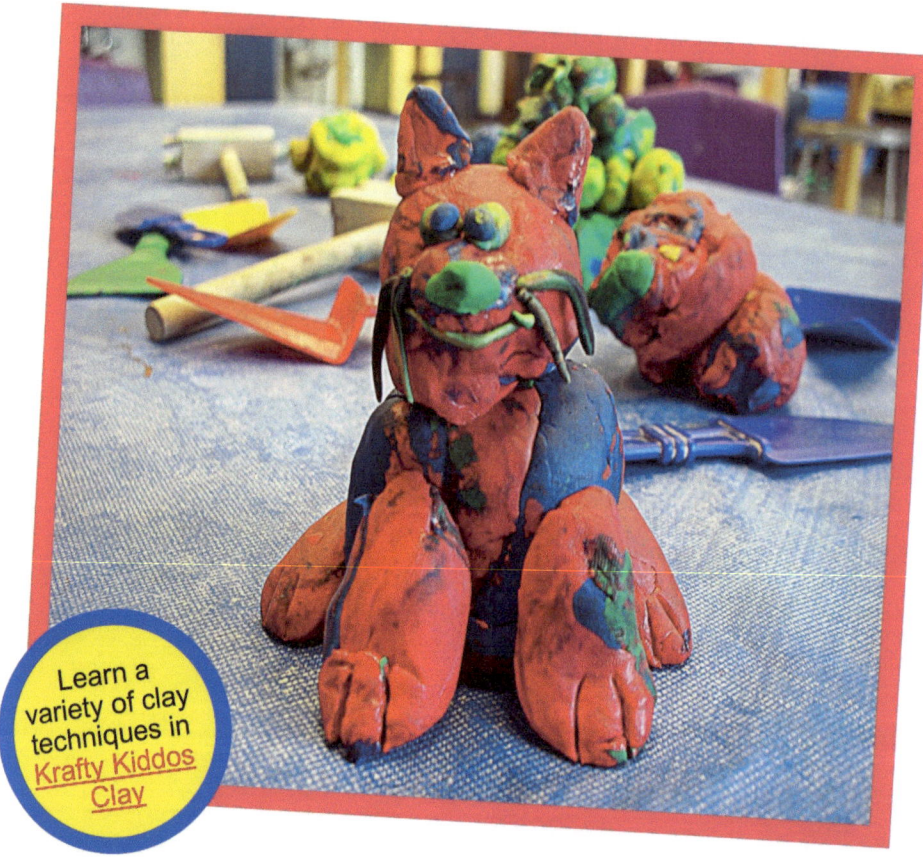

Learn a variety of clay techniques in Krafty Kiddos Clay

By age six, children are capable of learning to read and write music. They can focus on a single task for about fifteen minutes. They are indecisive, easily excitable, and often moody. Friendships are unstable day to day, but important.

Artwork often shows family and friends and basic geometric shapes are commonly used. Various techniques are explored including overlapping and shading and children enjoy discovering the full color spectrum.

Activities

Overlapping

Explore color mixing by overlapping different colors of paint, pencil, or crayon. Use light, gentle strokes and start with the lightest color first.

Wet Paper

Dampen a piece of paper with water then write on it with chalk and markers. The colors will pop and the edges will blur.

Clay

Unlike dough, modeling clay will not dry out. There are, however, air dry clays and ones you bake in ovens or kilns that will become hard.

Crayon Etching

Color hard with different colored crayons then color on top of that with black crayon. Use a paper clip to etch away a bright and colorful picture.

Watercolor Print

Dampen an absorbent piece of watercolor paper, drench it in watercolors, cover it with textured objects, add weight on top, and allow to dry.

PAPER CHAIN

Cut paper into strips then staple or glue the ends together to form links. Combine the links and decorate with paint, crayons, or odds and ends.

Lacing

Lace yarn and ribbon through hole punched paper. Try skipping holes, using multiple colors of yarn, spelling words, and numbers, etc.

Types of Paint

Explore all paint: tempera, puff, neon, watercolor, glitter, glow in the dark, magnetic, crackle, chalkboard, fabric, latex, and whiteboard-just to name a few!

Stocking

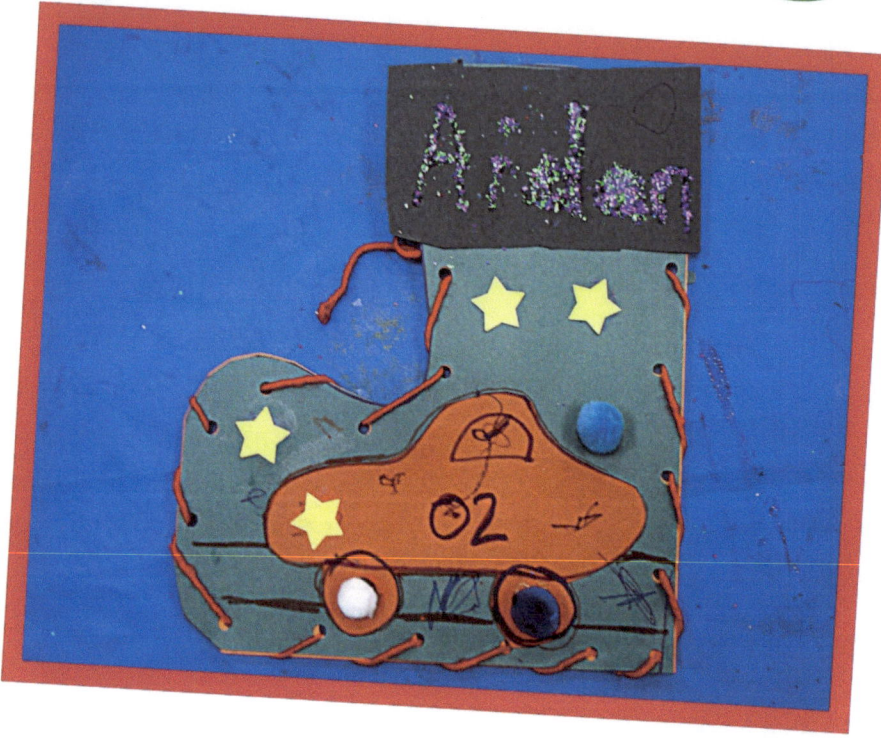

Try lacing the stocking with multiple colors of yarn or ribbon. Punch more holes or less depending on your preference.

Step 1	Draw a stocking outline on a sheet of paper
Step 2	Place another sheet of paper beneath it
Step 3	Cut around the outline
Step 4	Punch holes around the edge
Step 5	Lace the pieces together
Step 6	Tie a bow or knot at the end
Step 7	Decorate the stocking however you like

Paper Chain
FLAG

Step 1   Cut strips of blue, white, and red paper

Step 2   Glue the strips to form equal size links

Step 3   Glue the links to paper in the pattern below

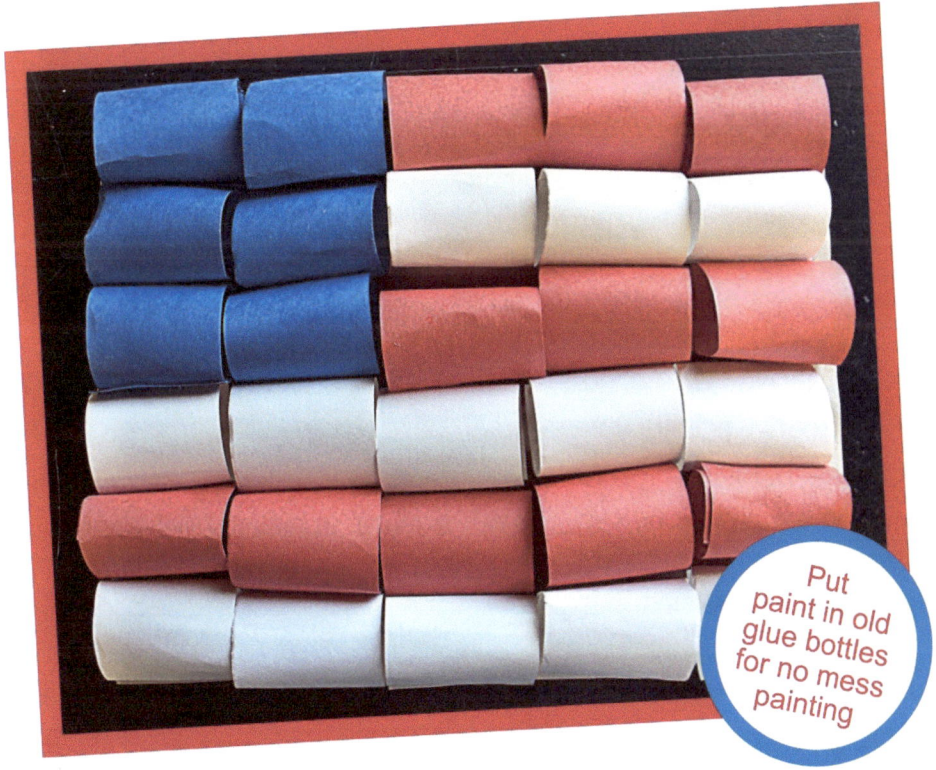

Put paint in old glue bottles for no mess painting

Color the paper prior to forming the links or decorate the flag as a whole at the end. Try splatter painting it or adding odds and ends or glitter.

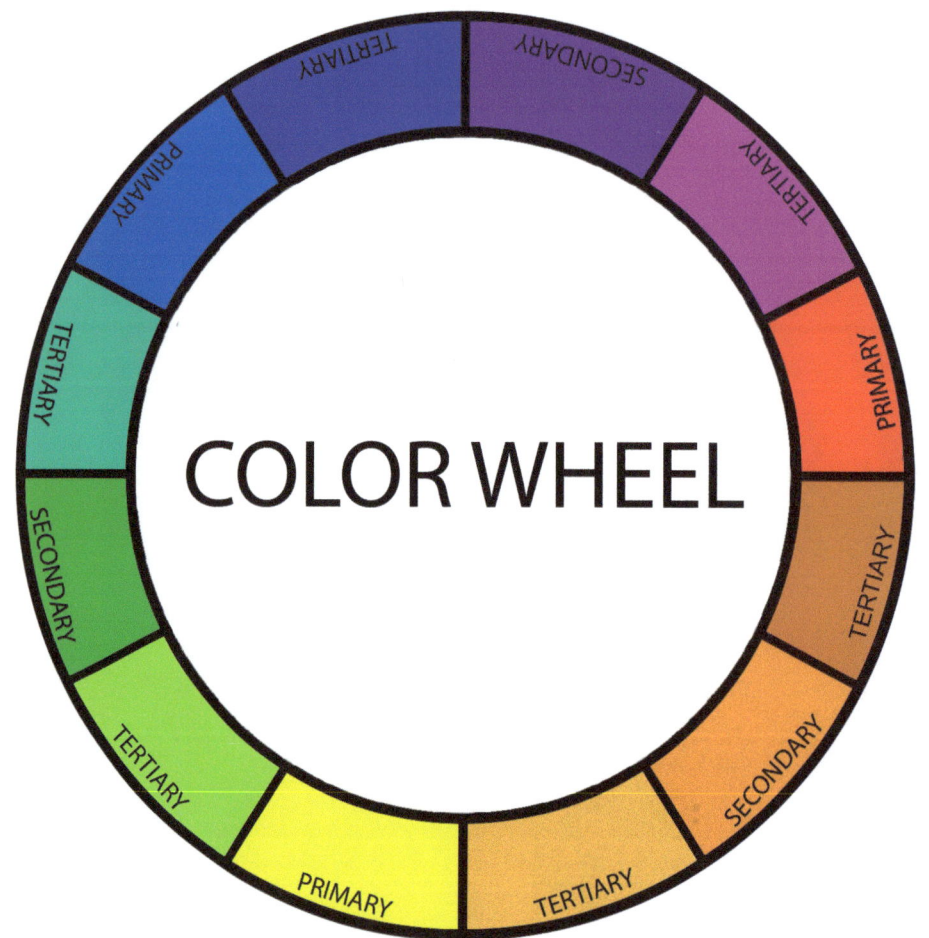

COLOR WHEEL

When mixing colors, always start with the lightest color first.

Red, yellow, and blue are considered primary colors because no other colors mix together to make them.

Secondary colors are an equal mix of two primary colors. Red and blue, for example, combine to make purple.

Tertiary colors are an un-equal mix of colors. More blue than red, for example, combines to make violet, a lighter shade of purple.

Study the color wheel above then make your own! Fold a paper plate again and again until you have twelve sections then paint each section a different color.

Body Outline

Step 1   Lie on the floor in a unique position

Step 2   Have a friend outline your body

Step 3   Decorate your body outline

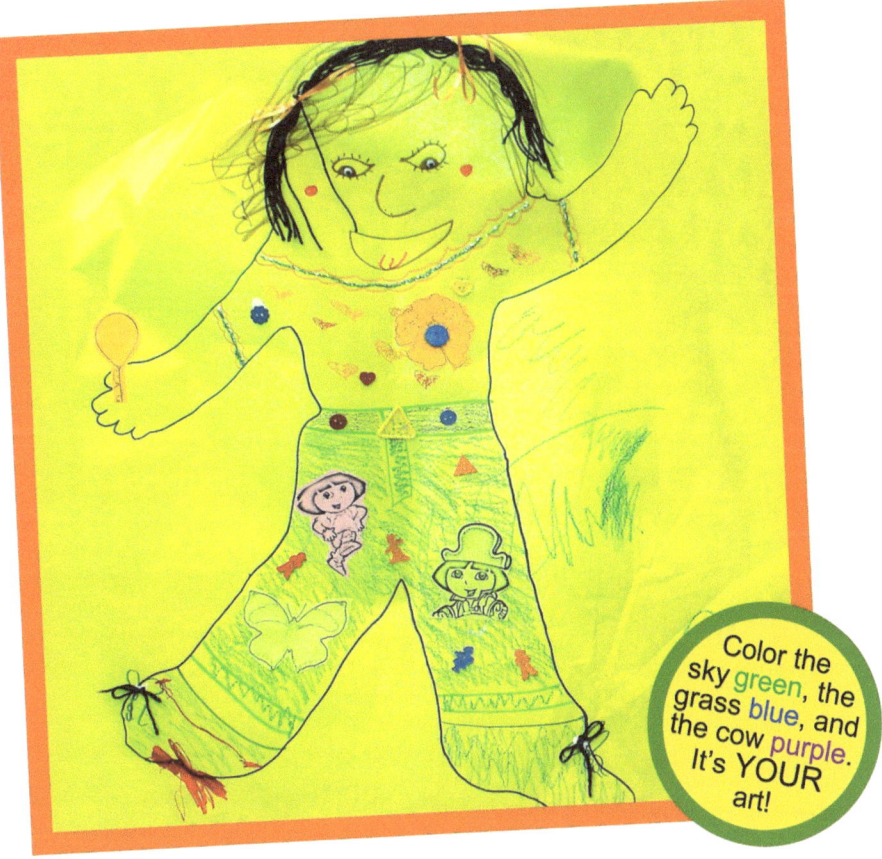

Color the sky green, the grass blue, and the cow purple. It's YOUR art!

Outline bodies onto butcher paper or simply lie down on the driveway and use chalk. Add details using yarn, buttons, and other odds and ends. Draw yourself in your favorite shirt or sports uniform, pose like a ballerina, or add a baseball glove to your hand. Give yourself crazy hair and add pets or friends to the picture. To learn about the body, draw the ribs, bones, and organs.

SEvEN Years

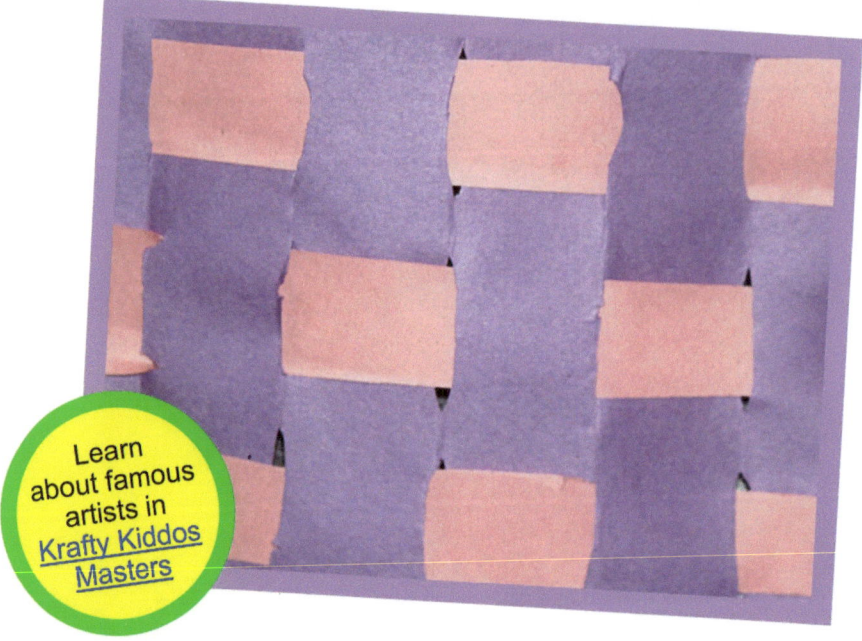

Learn about famous artists in Krafty Kiddos Masters

Seven year olds are more cooperative and dislike criticism. They want to be accepted by friends and are more grounded in reality than make believe. They enjoy hobbies and new challenges.

They express their feelings and ideas in their artwork and are interested in learning new techniques. Seven year olds notice the different body types of people and display that in their pictures. Their artwork reflects their life and they enjoy hearing stories of famous artists.

They think simply and can state why they like or dislike certain artwork (ex. "I like the blue in this picture"). They also understand that artwork affects people in different ways.

Activities

Dry Brush

Dip a dry paintbrush in a touch of paint then use on dry paper. The result is a rough, distressed texture perfect for painting tree bark, wind, etc.

Alcohol

Paint watercolors onto paper then drip alcohol onto the page for a stunning spotted effect. Use this technique to make stars or animal spots.

Bubble Paint

Mix paint, dishwashing liquid, and water together in a bowl. Blow through a straw to make bubbles then rest a piece of paper on top for a cool picture.

Eye Droppers

Drip different colored paint on a piece of paper using an eye dropper. Lift and turn the paper to create interesting abstract designs.

Weave

Fan fold a piece of paper and cut slits along the folds on both sides. Unfold the paper and weave colored strips of paper though the holes.

TRACING

Trace around cans, boxes, shoes, hands, etc. When you're done, add in the details like laces, rings, etc. or turn the shapes into other objects.

Paper Doll Chain

Fan fold paper and cut out a body. Leave the hands and feet uncut at the folds so when the paper is unfolded, the people are connected.

Color Block

Draw an object or a picture then divide it into sections with curved or straight lines. Color or paint each section a different color.

POP UP CARD

Step 1   Fold two pieces of paper in half

Step 2   Cut 1in. slits through the fold of one sheet

Step 3   Push the slits "out" instead of "in"

Step 4   Glue the sheets of paper together

Step 5   Put cutouts on the pop ups

Step 6   Decorate the rest of the card

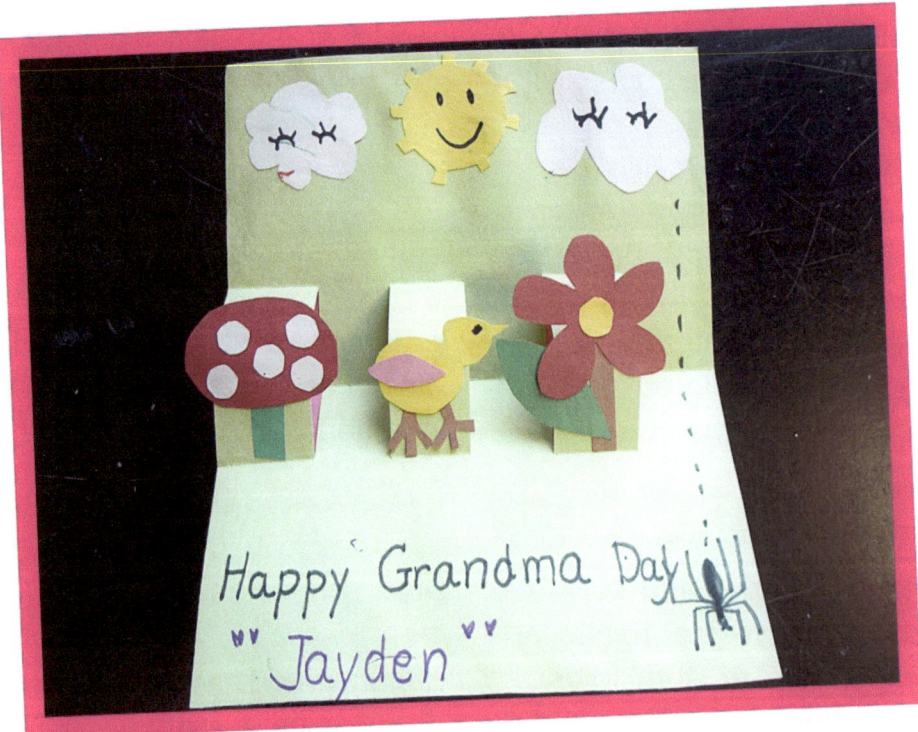

Try using the beads to make a necklace rather than a wreath.

Paper Beads

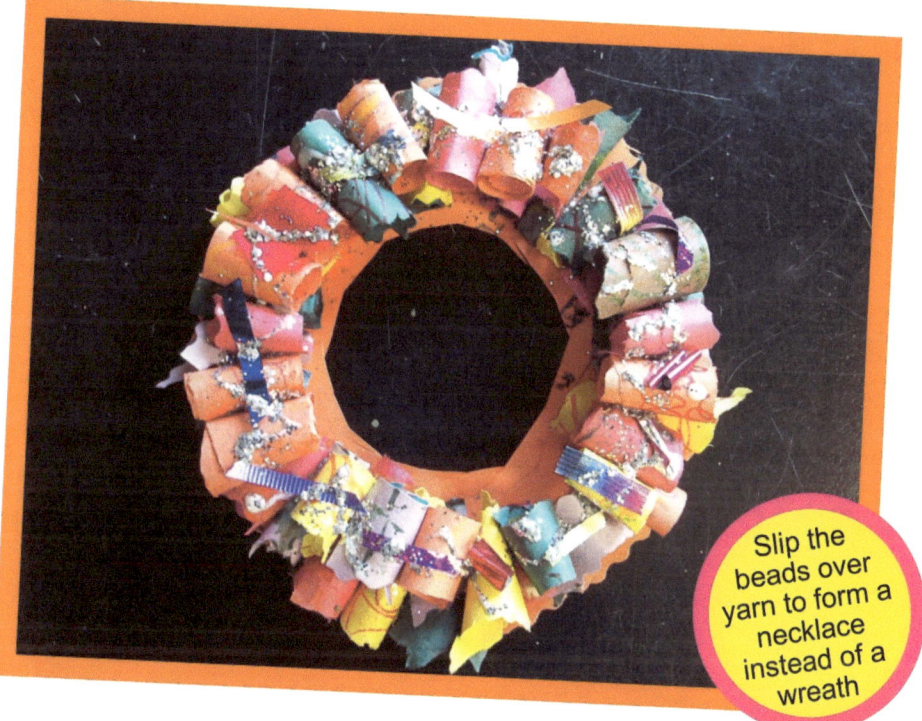

Slip the beads over yarn to form a necklace instead of a wreath

Use cardstock or cardboard to form a more sturdy wreath

Step 1   Cut a wreath shape out of paper

Step 2   Tear scrap paper into strips

Step 3   Wrap each strip around a fat marker

Step 4   Glue the end down

Step 5   Pull paper bead off the marker

Step 6   Glue beads to the paper wreath

Step 7   Decorate with odds and ends and glitter

Layered Picture

Step 1   Draw a picture to use as a guide

Step 2   Cut out objects that match the picture

Step 3   Outline the objects in black (optional)

Step 4   Arrange the objects over the drawing

Step 5   Glue them down, bottom to top

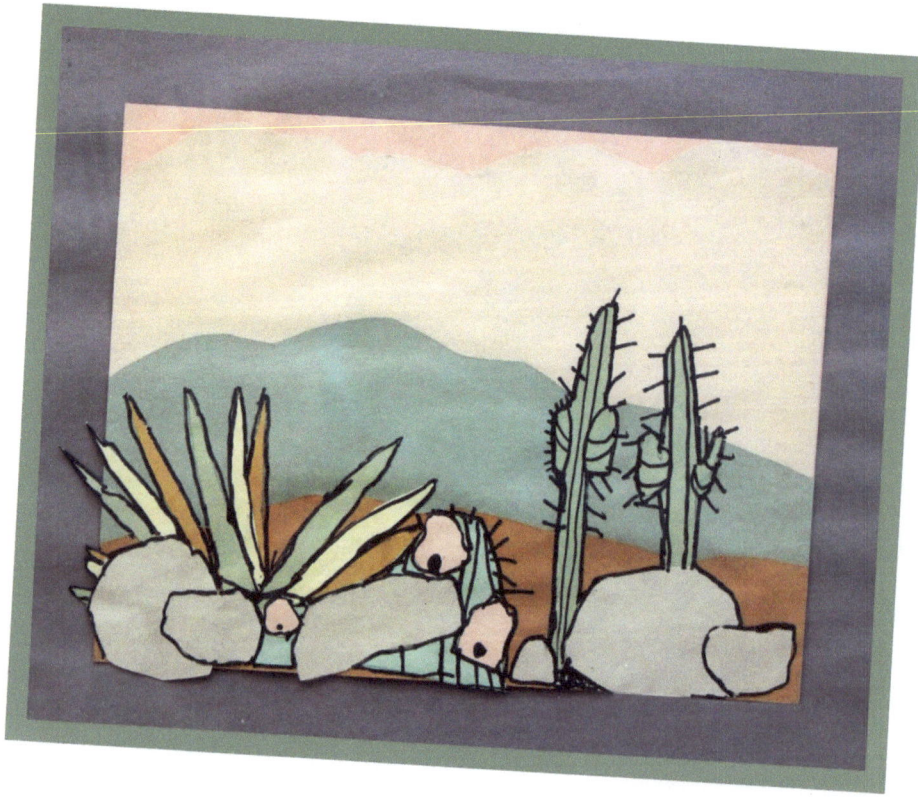

Layered pictures are not limited to landscapes

Tracing

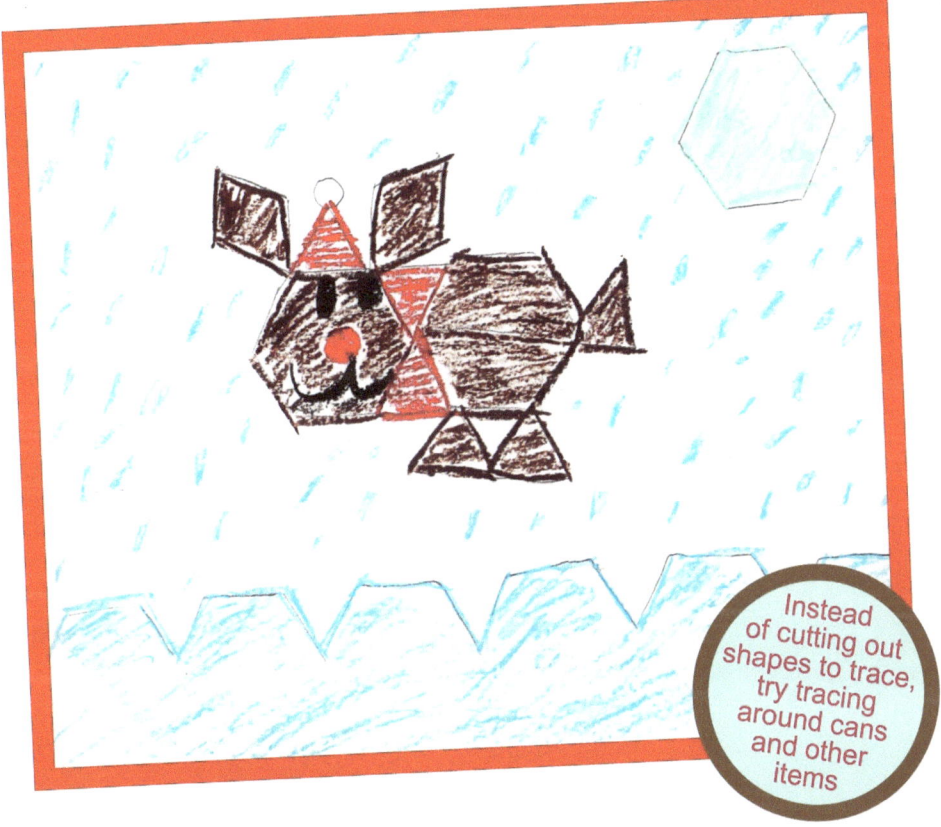

Instead of cutting out shapes to trace, try tracing around cans and other items

Sharpen your math skills! Assign point values to each shape then try to create a picture that totals a specific amount.

Step 1   Cut out a variety of shapes

Step 2   Trace around them to form a picture

Step 3   Color

Step 4   Add odds and ends (optional)

EiGHt Years

Eight year olds are anxious to learn. They have good attention spans and understand best when ideas are related to real life. They seek out a best friend, often have heroes, and prefer to play with children of the same gender. They are very critical of themselves and others. Eight year olds have a strong desire for independence, but a reliance on adults for protection.

They like to draw subjects in motion and are interested in learning more complex techniques. Drawings are detailed with people typically having an average of ten features.

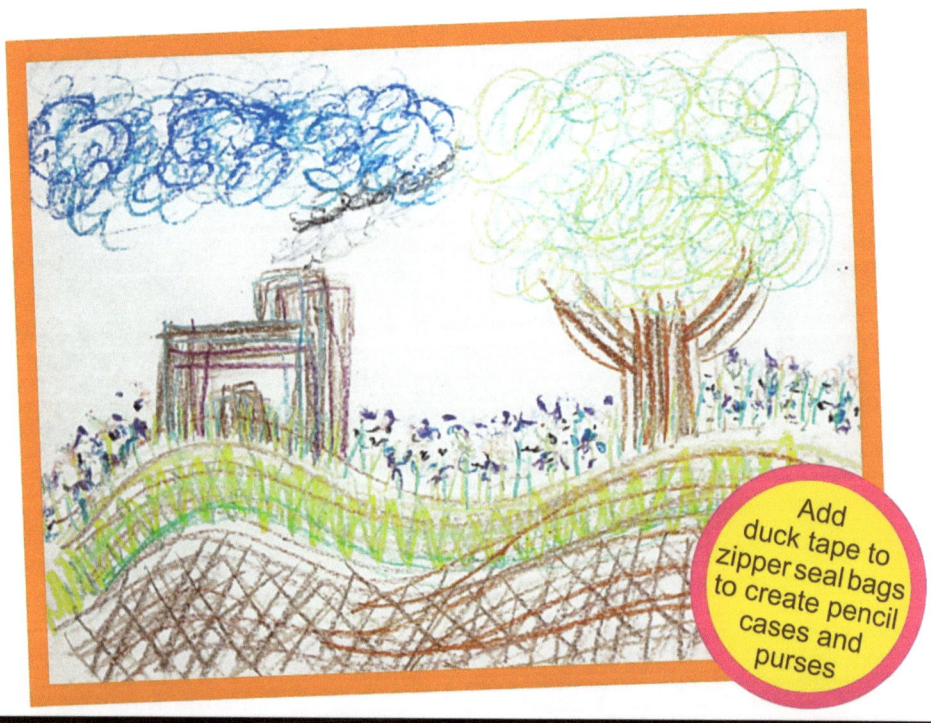

Add duck tape to zipper seal bags to create pencil cases and purses

Activities

Finish The Drawing

Draw random lines and shapes on a piece of paper then find a way to combine them to form a cohesive picture.

Duck Tape

Use duck tape to make a variety of crafts such as pencil cases, wallets, headbands, and more! It comes in all different colors and designs.

Stippling

Dip the tips of a dry paintbrush in paint then tap them on paper for a stippling effect. Create an entire picture this way or use it to make snow or freckles!

Multiple Crayons

Tape several crayons together to create multi-line drawings. Use this technique with pencils, pens, or markers as well.

Continuous Drawing

Try drawing a picture without lifting your pencil. Add challenge by not retracing lines. An Etch-A-Sketch is a great way to practice this technique.

DIORAMA

Turn an empty shoe box into a diorama by turning it on it's side and filling it with various objects that create a scene from history or a book.

Stencils

Stencils are a fun way to create pictures and a useful tool for making posters. They come in all different shapes and sizes.

Tissue Paper

Cut tissue paper into squares and glue flat or crumbled onto paper. Glue to wax paper to make sun catchers or fold whole sheets to make flowers.

Tissue Flower

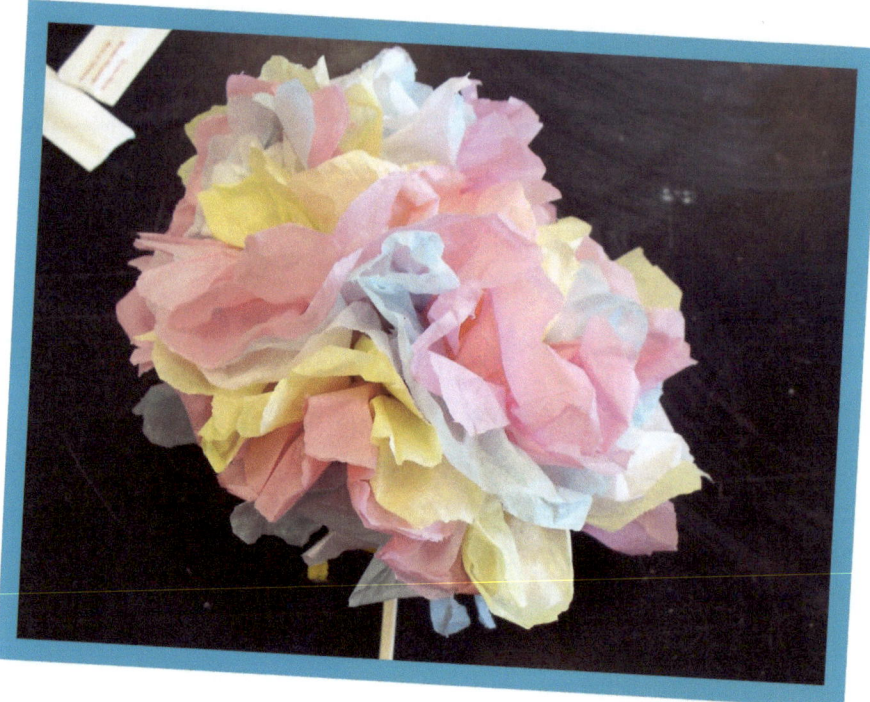

Variations: (1) Make the center a different color by adding an accordion folded contrasting color of tissue paper on top of the stack after step two. (2) Cut the sheets pointy or rounded while stacked for different looks. (3) Tape wire or a chopstick to the flower during step 4 to create a stem. (4) Use half or quarter sheets of tissue paper for smaller flowers. (5) Use newspaper rather than tissue paper then decorate with paint, glitter, etc.

Step 1   Stack 3 or more sheets of tissue paper

Step 2   Fan fold the stack

Step 3   Fold the stack in half

Step 4   Squeeze the middle and tape it tightly

Step 5   Unfold the tissue paper to form a flower

Step 6   Maneuver the paper to fill any gaps

Salt Chalk

Step 1   Pour a small amount of salt into a bowl
Step 2   Rotate a piece of chalk around the bowl
Step 3   Pour the newly colored salt into the jar
Step 4   Tap the jar so the salt will settle
Step 5   Repeat the process, layering the colors
Step 6   Continue filling and tapping until jar is full
Step 7   Attach lid

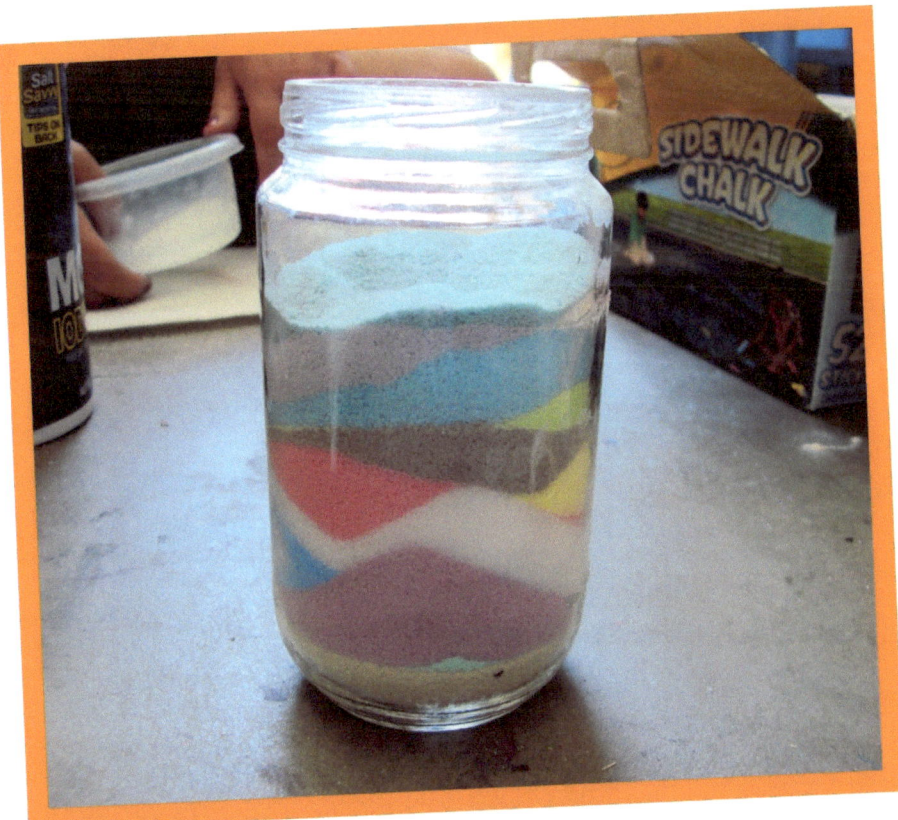

Slide a skewer down the sides of the jar to form designs in the salt

Elephant

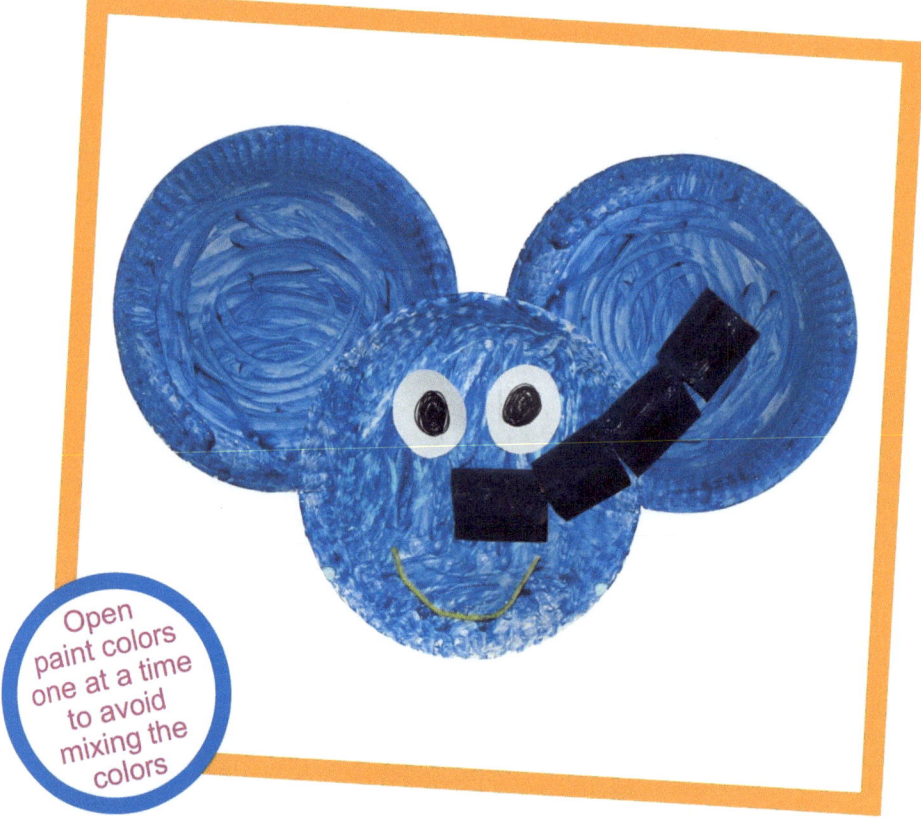

Open paint colors one at a time to avoid mixing the colors

Insert pipe cleaner through rolls and attach to plate for a movable nose.

Step 1   Cut two or three toilet paper rolls in half

Step 2   Staple two paper plates on top (ears)

Step 3   Glue rolls to paper plate (nose)

Step 4   Paint and decorate your elephant

FRIENDSHIP *Bracelets*

Step 1	Cut three equal length pieces of yarn
Step 2	Tie them together on one side
Step 3	Name the strands 1, 2, and 3
Step 4	Put strand 1 over 2 and under 3
Step 5	Put strand 2 over 3 and under 1
Step 6	Put strand 3 over 1 and under 2
Step 7	Repeat this process, pulling tightly
Step 8	Tie the ends together to form bracelet

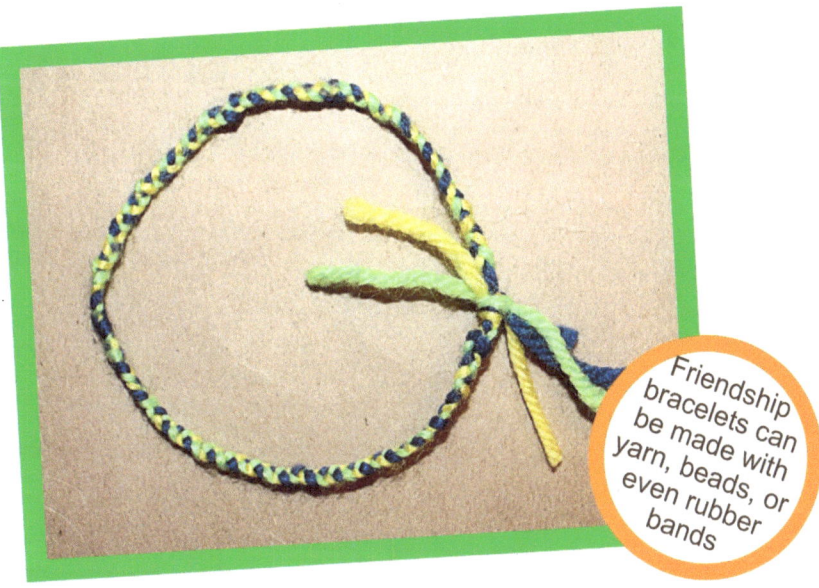

Friendship bracelets can be made with yarn, beads, or even rubber bands

Using different colors of yarn makes braiding easier. Always braid in the same order (ex. blue, green, yellow... blue, green, yellow, etc.). Use more yarn to make thicker bracelets and longer pieces to make necklaces.

Nine Years

Nine year olds have a lively curiosity, lots of interests, and a love of adventure and competition. They like group and club activities but are also independent. They are dependable and trustworthy, and typically take responsibility for their actions.

Nine year olds display more abstract reasoning skills and individual differences are more noticeable. They have an attention span that lasts about one hour. They enjoy collecting things and learning about the world around them.

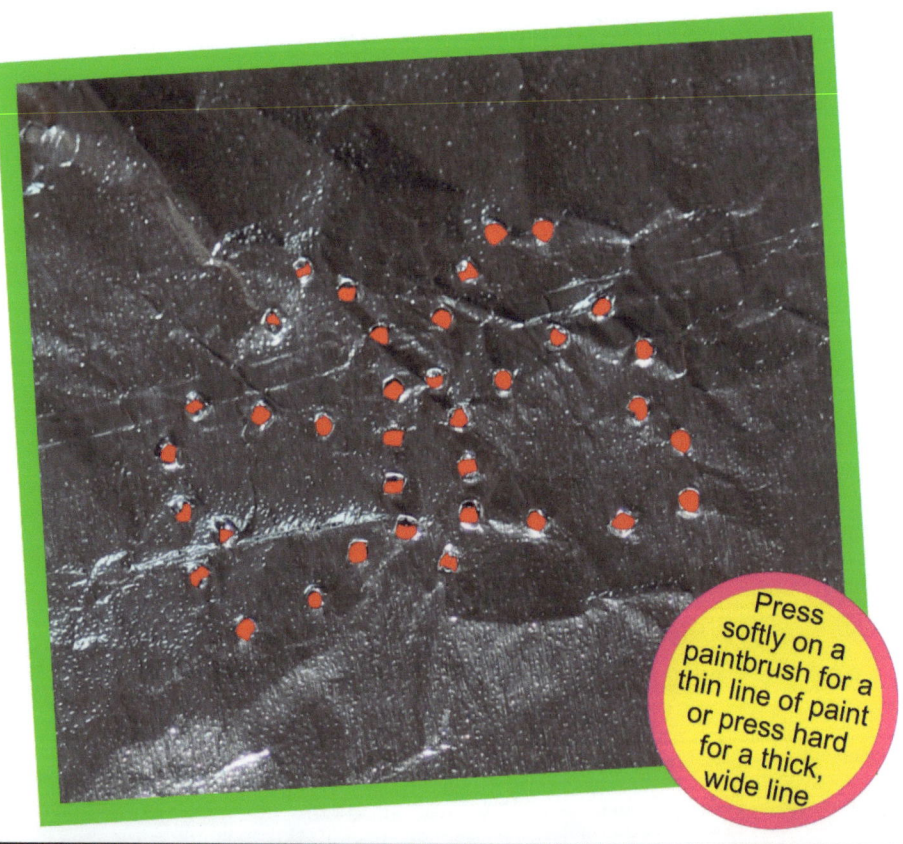

Press softly on a paintbrush for a thin line of paint or press hard for a thick, wide line

Activities

Double Paint

Dip each half of your paint-brush in a different color. Try using complementary colors, shades of the same color, or contrasting colors.

Straw Paint

Drip watered down paint onto a sheet of paper then blow through a drinking straw to direct the paint in different directions.

Mixing Mediums

Mixing mediums can be added to paint to add texture, shimmer, etc. There are even products that turn normal paint into fabric paint!

Watercolor Pencils

Draw as you would with colored pencils, but when done, brush over the picture with water and watch the colors run together like paint!

Textured Paint

Paint a picture then sprinkle different textured material onto the page. Try using sand for a desert landscape or crushed leaves for a forest.

Paper Maché

Make piñatas and assorted art pieces through paper maché. Run strips of paper through a mixture of flour and water then place atop a form.

Hole Punch

Use a pen to make a design in dots on a piece of foil. Lift the foil and punch a pen tip through the holes. Try using a coloring book picture as a guide.

Splatter Paint

Flick toothbrush or paintbrush bristles with your finger. It's VERY messy and may be difficult for toddlers. Use lots of newspaper or do it outside.

Crazy Hat

Step 1   Turn a grocery bag upside down

Step 2   Size it to fit the head

Step 3   Roll the bottom up to form a brim

Step 4   Decorate the hat however you like

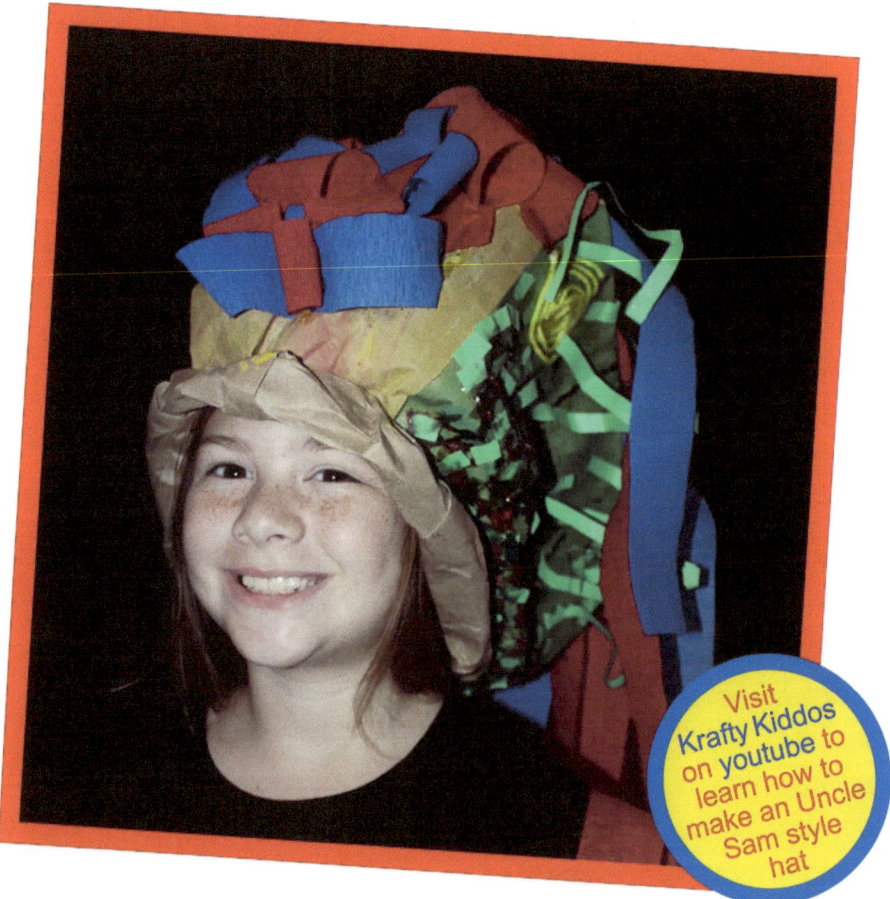

Visit Krafty Kiddos on youtube to learn how to make an Uncle Sam style hat

Fill a bin with random odds and ends like crepe paper, stickers, markers, tape, glue, scissors, glitter, wrapping paper, etc. for decorating your hat.

Yarn Bowl

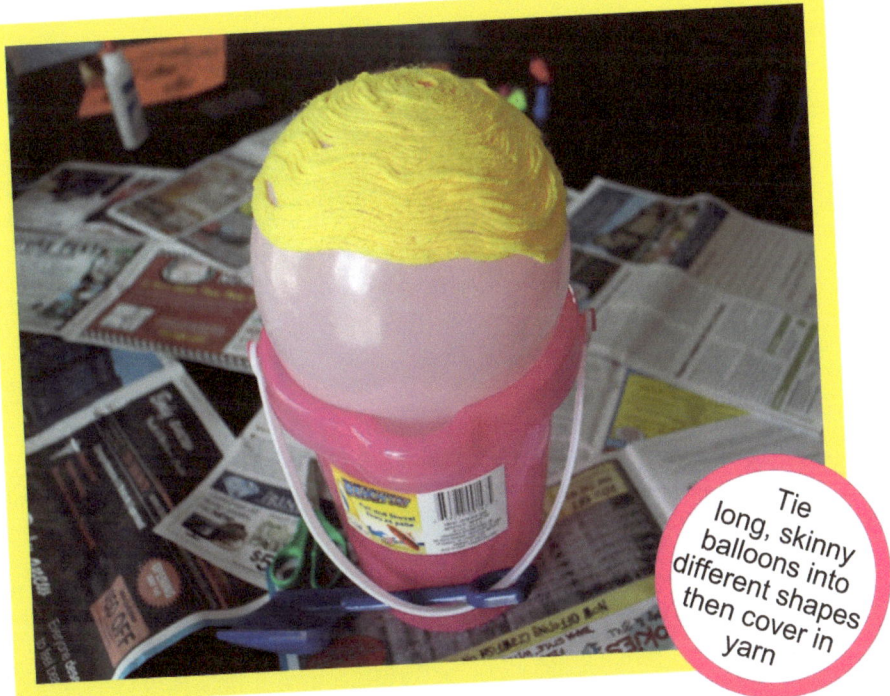

Tie long, skinny balloons into different shapes then cover in yarn

Make the sides straight or wavy. Try using different colored yarn.

Step 1   Blow up a balloon

Step 2   Place it upside down in a bucket or bowl

Step 3   Mix white glue and a little water in a bowl

Step 4   Run pieces of yarn through the mixture

Step 5   Place yarn onto the balloon

Step 6   Form a bowl shape

Step 7   Allow to dry

Step 8   Remove and use

Scribble Designs

Step 1   Scribble haphazardly
Step 2   Fill open spaces with colors or designs

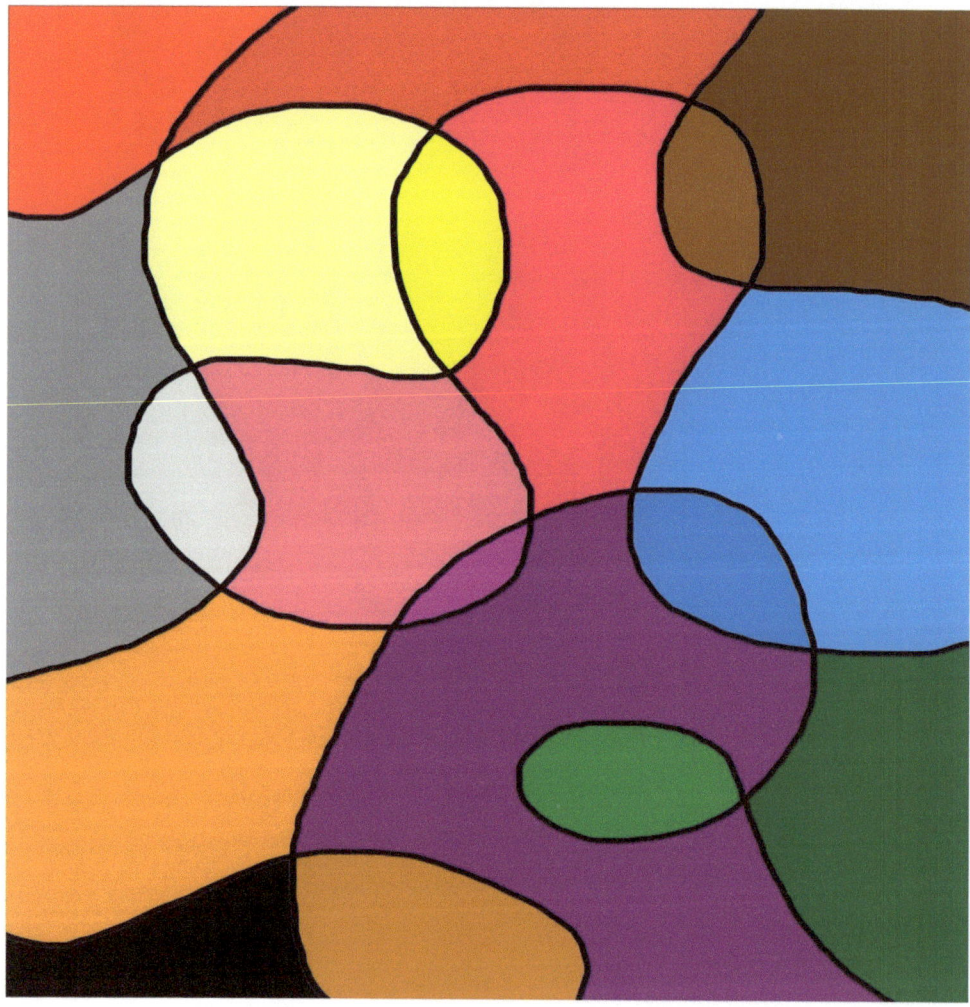

Explore colors, shades, lines, patterns, textures, and space all in one project! Use crayons, markers, paint, chalk, pastels… or even a computer. The picture above was created on a laptop using Photoshop.

Photo Transfer

Step 1   Flatten polymer clay

Step 2   Place a xerox picture onto the clay

Step 3   Dampen with alcohol soaked cotton ball

Step 4   Rub for several minutes with a spoon

Step 5   Remove the picture from the clay

Step 6   Cut around the clay and bake

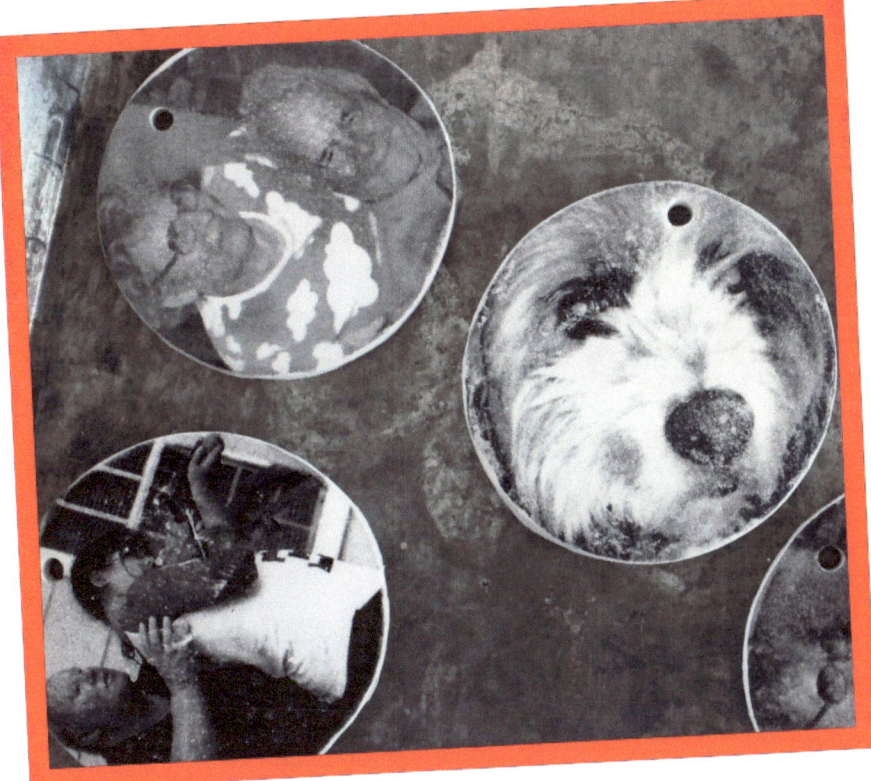

Pictures must be xeroxed and not printed on an inkjet printer. Note that any words will appear backward in the clay. Cans can be used to cut shapes and straws can be used to cut holes for hanging.

TeN Years

Friendships are very important to ten year olds and the opinions of friends may mean more than the opinions of parents. Kids this age can be sensitive, uncooperative, irritable, and rude, but are more often polite, honest, and easy going. They also may try to hide their problems.

As their brains continue to develop, their artistic ability grows. They are capable of understanding more complicated concepts and techniques. They have better control over their small muscles and can draw and write more precisely. They like to be challenged and are enthusiastic about learning new things.

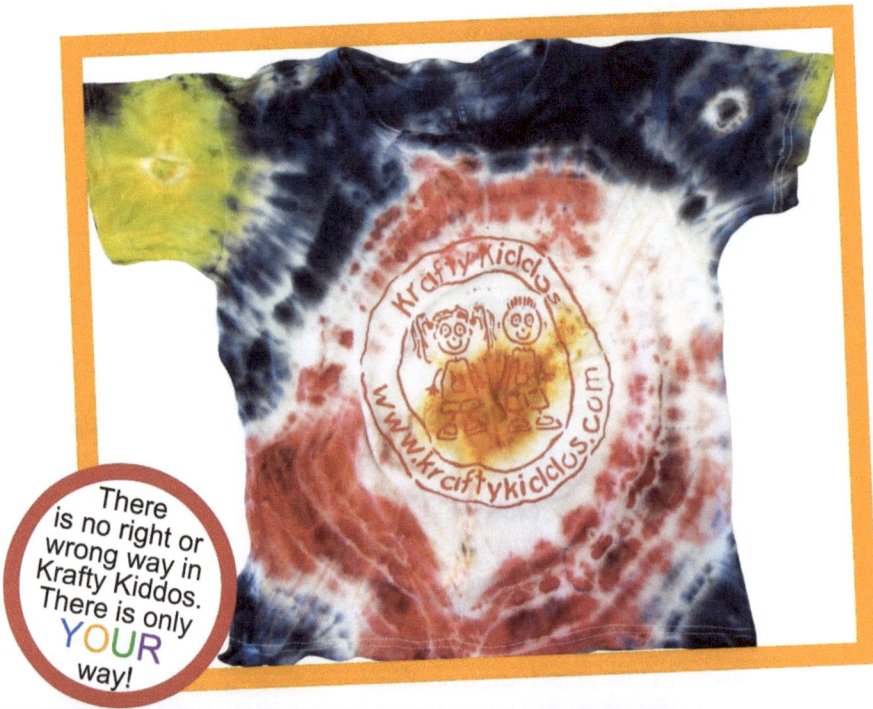

There is no right or wrong way in Krafty Kiddos. There is only YOUR way!

Activities

Paper Sculpture

Twist newspaper into various shapes then paint. Connect pieces using tape. Create hats, animals, people, flames, trees, words, and more.

Animation

Draw a very basic picture on a piece of paper. On subsequent pages, draw slight movement to the picture. Flip the pages to see your animation.

Warm & Cool

Draw a simple picture twice - once with only cool colors (greens, blues, violets) and again with only warm colors (reds, oranges, yellows).

Tie Dye

Fold material then tie with rubber bands and submerge in dye to create unique and eye catching designs. The trick is in the way you tie it!

Hard & Soft

Paint or draw a picture using both hard edges (very distinct edges) and soft edges (edges that fade into the background with no distinct boundary).

Geometric Designs

Use rulers, protractors, and compasses to make overlapping geometric designs. Try black and white or color and use pencils or ink.

CROSS STITCH

Use a needle and thread on a piece of cross stitch fabric to create different designs. Cheap kits are sold in stores or draw your own design.

Color Blending

Use blending pencils, cloths, and even your fingers to blend pencil, chalk, pastels, and crayons. It adds value and shine to your pictures.

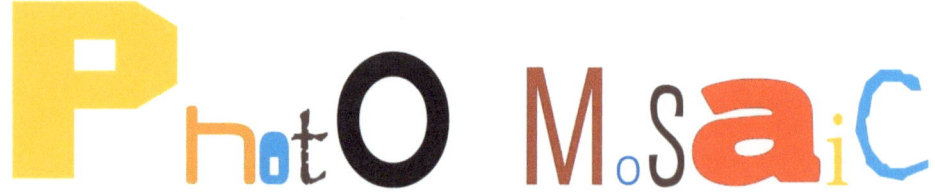

Photo Mosaic

Step 1   Print or draw a picture
Step 2   Cut it into squares
Step 3   Mix the squares up
Step 4   Randomly glue them to a sheet of paper

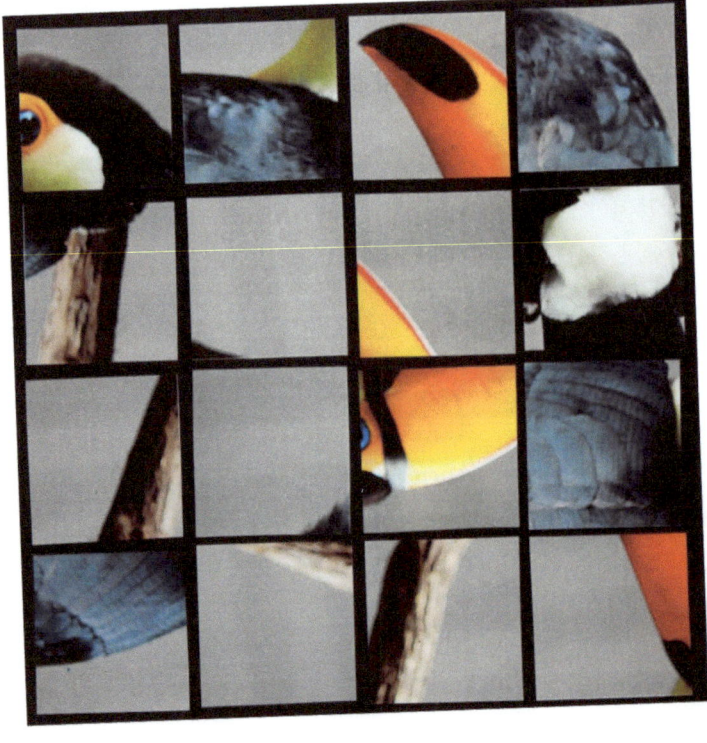

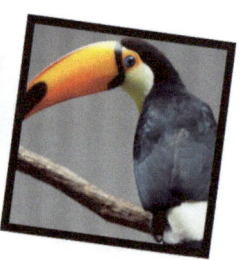

Mix the pieces up or glue them in the correct order, whichever you prefer.
Try cutting the pieces in different sizes and shapes or gluing them to dif-
ferent colors of paper. Add glitter between the pictures or raise some or all
of them off the page with foam adhesive. There are endless possibilities!

Calligraphy

Calligraphy is a beautiful writing style that has been used around the world for hundreds of years. It is often used on invitations and diplomas. There are different styles of calligraphy ranging from very simple to very ornate. There are also different pens specifically used in calligraphy.

Below are several calligraphy styles for you to try. Which is the easiest? Which is your favorite?

Aa Bb Cc Dd Ee Ff Gg Hh Ii Jj Kk Ll Mm Nn Oo Pp Qq Rr Ss Tt Uu Vv Ww Xx Yy Zz 0123456789

Aa Bb Cc Dd Ee Ff Gg Hh Ii Jj Kk Ll Mm Nn Oo Pp Qq Rr Ss Tt Uu Vv Ww Xx Yy Zz 0123456789

Aa Bb Cc Dd Ee Ff Gg Hh Ii Jj Kk Ll Mm Nn Oo Pp Qq Rr Ss Tt Uu Vv Ww Xx Yy Zz 0123456789

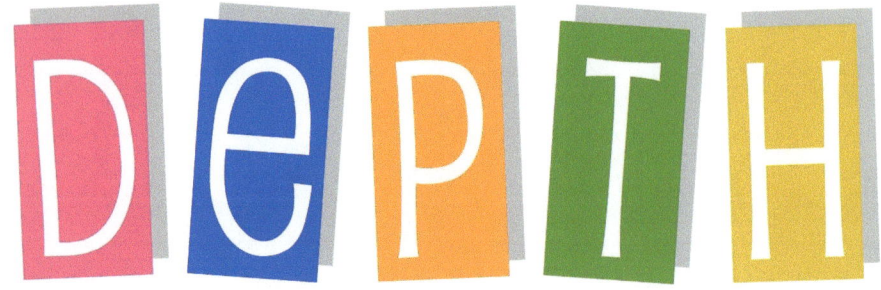

Step 1   Draw a word or shape

Step 2   Select a point to be the vanishing point

Step 3   Draw lines toward that point

Step 4   Shade the area dark to light

Step 5   Fill the word with color or design (optional)

Try to create a full page of overlapping 3d shapes and figures

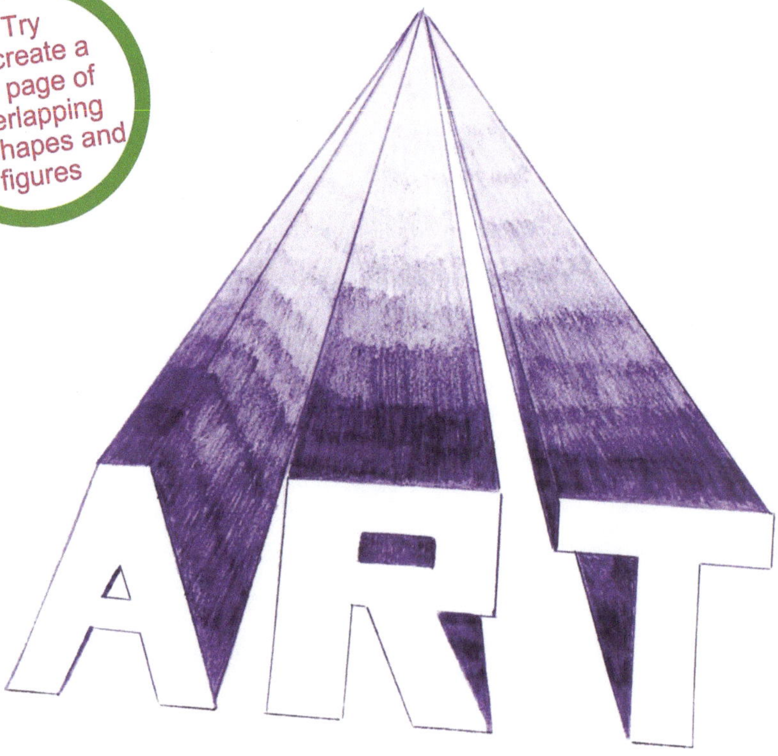

A ruler is helpful, but not necessary. Use colors or simply grey tone.

Shades

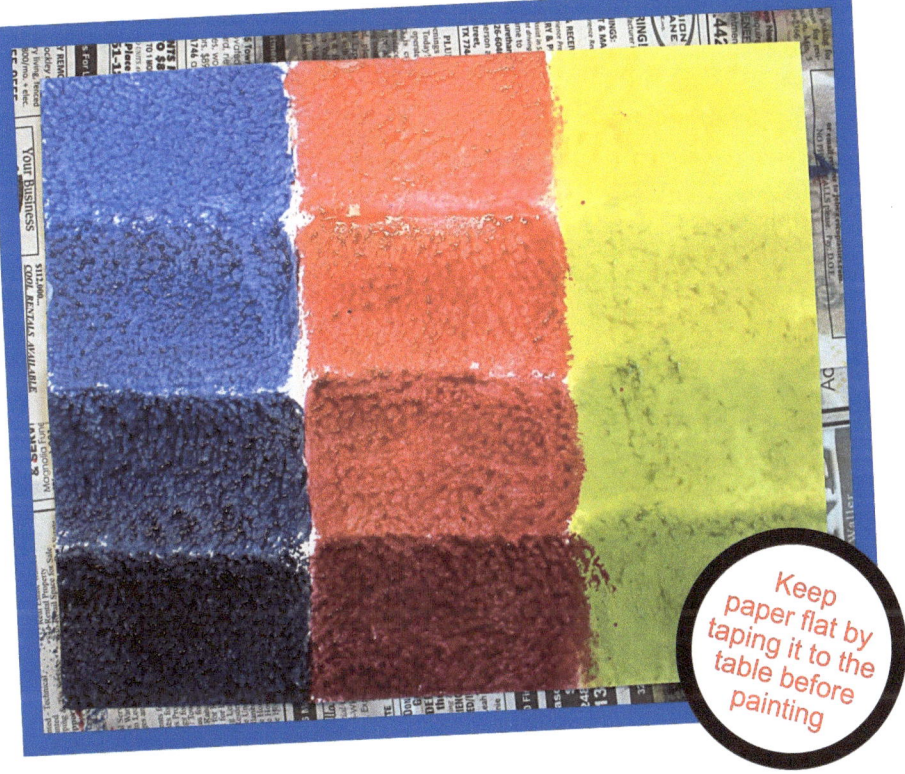

When colors are mixed together, the result is a brand new color. Red and yellow combine to make orange for example. But when white or black are added to a color, the result is simply a lighter or darker shade. Do this project using black or white paint and use brushes or sponges.

Keep paper flat by taping it to the table before painting

Step 1	Fold paper to form 3 columns and 4 rows
Step 3	Paint top squares red, yellow, and blue
Step 4	Add more black paint to each row
Step 5	Repeat until all squares are painted

EleVen Years

Eleven year olds are becoming more serious. They are considering future careers and their shift is away from play and toward academics. They are very competitive and more interested in current events than in history.

Eleven year olds love a good story, whether it's based in reality or fantasy. They think more abstractly and can create art more quickly and precisely. They are more confident in their abilities and are always looking to advance them.

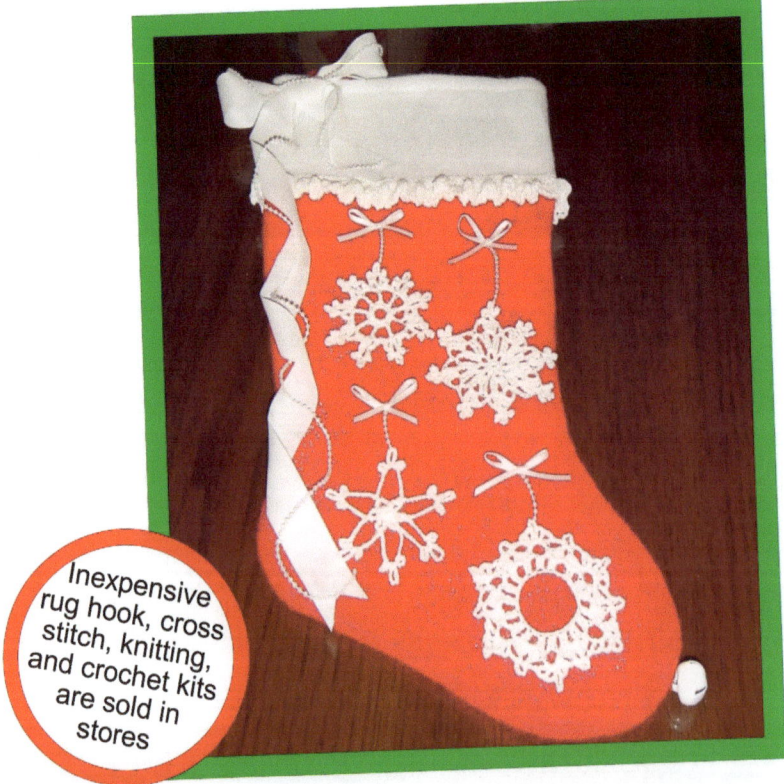

Inexpensive rug hook, cross stitch, knitting, and crochet kits are sold in stores

Activities

Wood Burning

Words and pictures can be burned into wood using special wood burning instruments. Kits often come with an assortment of tips.

Origami

Origami is the art of folding paper in different ways to create familiar or beautiful objects. Make animals, bowls, birds, and more!

Wire Sculpture

Wire comes in all different thicknesses and colors. What can you shape a piece of wire into? Let your creativity run wild!

Crochet

With yarn and a couple crochet needles, you can make a variety of beautiful pieces including afghans, scarves, hats, and gloves.

Soap Carving

Soap is a soft material that is easy to shape. Use a knife, exacto knife, scissors, sand paper, pencil, or paper clip for carving and etching.

SKETCH

Instead of drawing a shape with a single line, try sketching it using multiple loose, overlapping lines. Practice by sketching circles.

Plaster

Mix plaster with water and pour into molds to create hard, paintable pieces. Plaster will thicken and heat during the chemical transformation.

One Color Art

Try creating an entire picture using only shades of one color. Draw a tree with only shades of green or a dog with only shades of brown.

CRAYONS

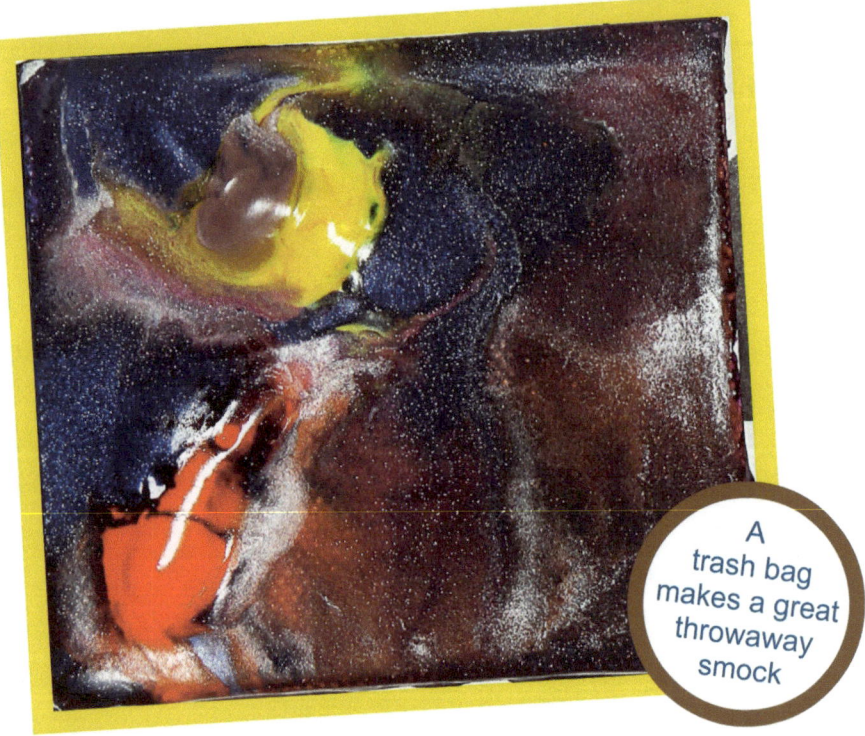

A trash bag makes a great throwaway smock

Leave some of the crayons partially melted to create rises and dips. Use sparkle crayons to add glitter to your finished work.

Step 1   Place a canvas on top of newspaper

Step 2   Select broken crayons

Step 3   Unpeel the labels

Step 4   Scatter them around a canvas

Step 5   Heat them with a hair dryer

Step 6   Rock the canvas to direct the wax

Step 7   Allow to dry then hang

Thread Designs

Step 1   Using a ruler, draw a square

Step 2   Mark every quarter of an inch

Step 3   Poke a hole on each mark with a needle

Step 4   Tie a knot in the thread at the beginning

Step 5   Run the thread in any pattern

Step 6   When you reach the end, tie a knot

Step 7   Repeat the process with different colors

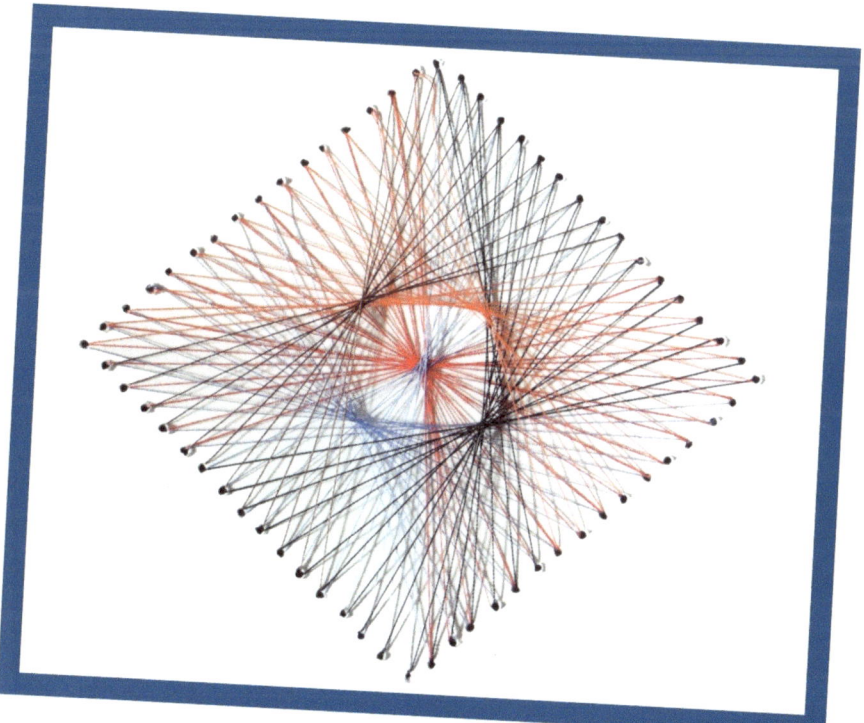

Create different designs and use as many or as few colors as you like.
Use poster board or try making a larger design on canvas to hang.

Distort & EXAGGERATE

Step 1   Determine an object to be the focal point

Step 2   Draw it in an exaggerated or distorted way

Step 3   Add more distorted objects to the picture

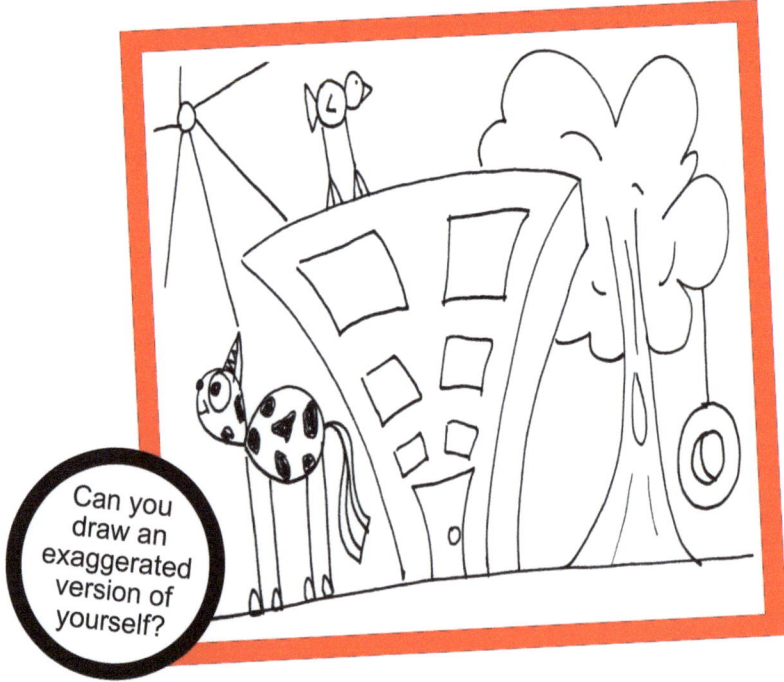

Can you draw an exaggerated version of yourself?

Make straight lines curvy and curvy lines straight. Add unusual height or proportion. Make butterflies bigger than houses. Remove all logic and reason. The more unusual, the better!

2 for 1

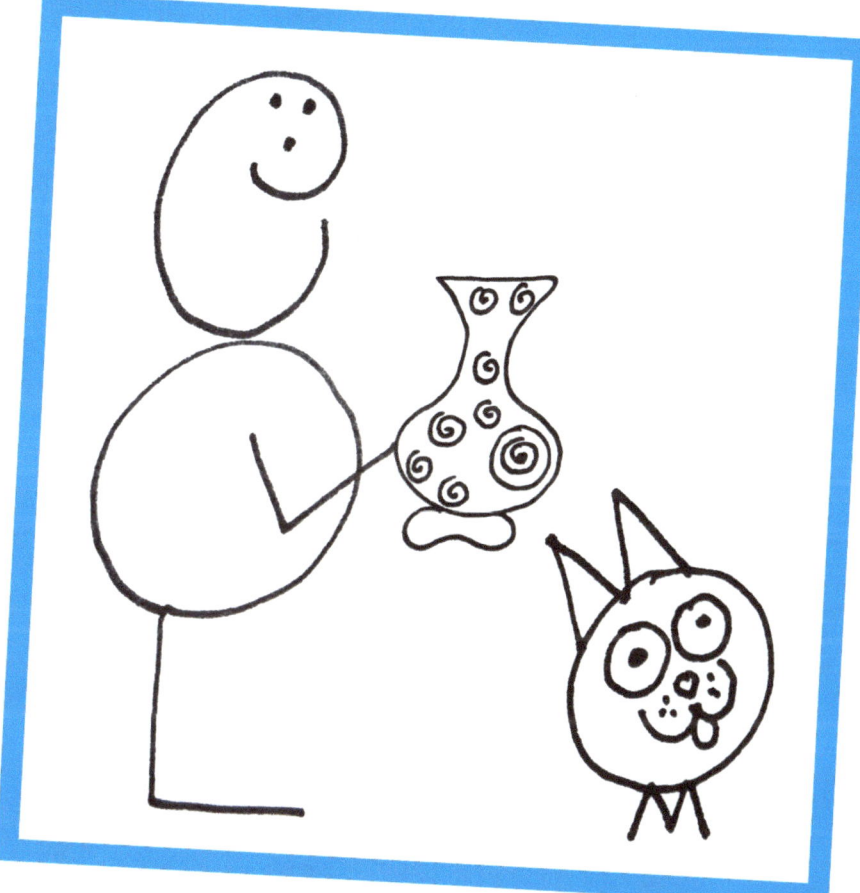

Can you see the hidden picture within each picture above? The stick person is made from the letters LOVE and the dog is made from the letters MOM. Look at the vase closely and you might see a fish!

Step 1   Think of a simple object to draw

Step 2   Consider how to draw it using letters

Step 3   Alternatively, draw two pictures in one

TweLVe Years

Twelve year olds can be emotional and rebellious. They test authority and have a growing need for independence. Their primary focus is on friends and school and they enjoy socializing in groups or pairs. They often work at developing a single, specific skill. Twelve year olds have a growing eye for detail and enjoy exploring new and different art ideas and techniques. They are creative and like to invent unusual things from raw materials. Their view of art continues to expand and may include methods new to them such as ceramics, sewing, or computer graphics.

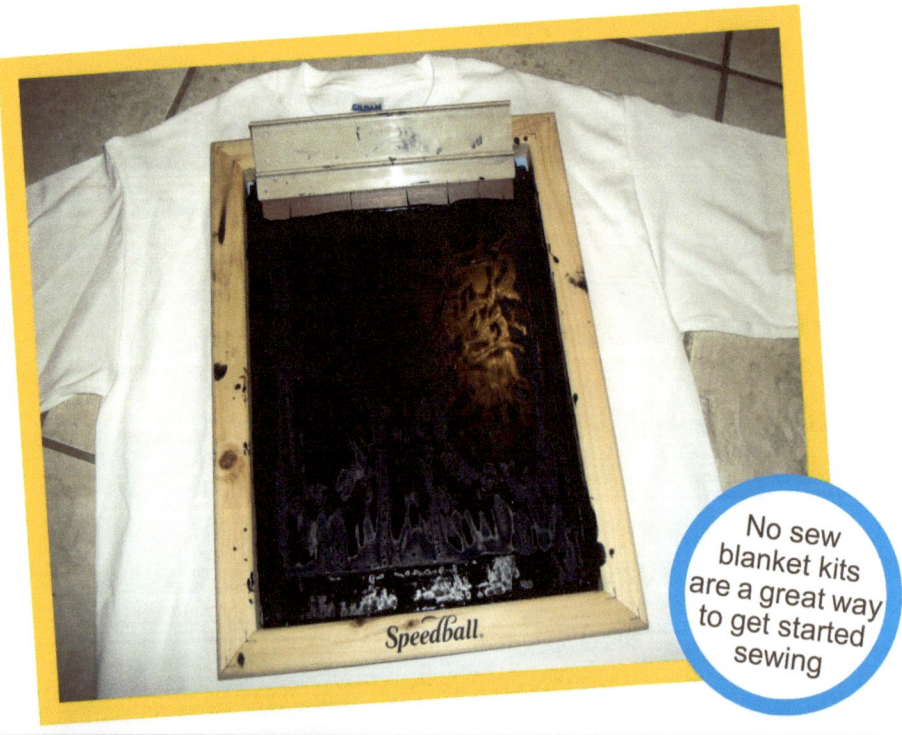

No sew blanket kits are a great way to get started sewing

Activities

Deconstruct

Look at a person or photo and try to deconstruct his or her face into simple shapes. The result will be a beautiful abstract portrait.

Mosaics

Glue stones, gems, etc. to an object, let it dry, then add grout. You can turn cans, pots, bottles, trays, and a host of other items into mosaics.

Color In 3D

Create a picture with LOTS of color then put on 3D glasses. Do any of the colors pop out? Try using yellows, oranges, and light blues and greens.

Perspective

Draw an object from different views. Try drawing a tall building straight on, from the top looking down, and from the bottom looking up.

Sewing

You don't need a sewing machine to sew. Cut some material and make a simple stocking or bag by hand. Try creating your own patterns.

Make Soap

Heat ingredients and pour into molds to create soap. Craft stores have all the materials. It is a simple process, but requires high heat.

Screen Print

Screen printing is the transfer of an image onto another surface such as paper or fabric. There are several ways to screen print.

Computer Graphics

Make the unreal appear real! Create stunning graphics using simple photo editing software. Many programs are inexpensive or even free.

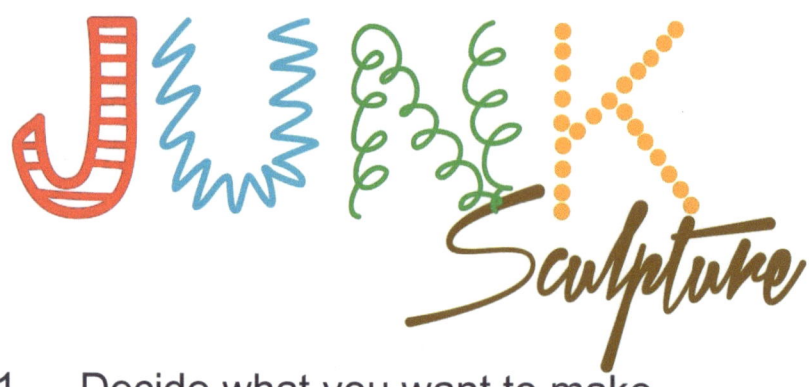

JUNK Sculpture

Step 1 Decide what you want to make
Step 2 Collect junk from around the house
Step 3 Heat up a hot glue gun
Step 4 Attach the items

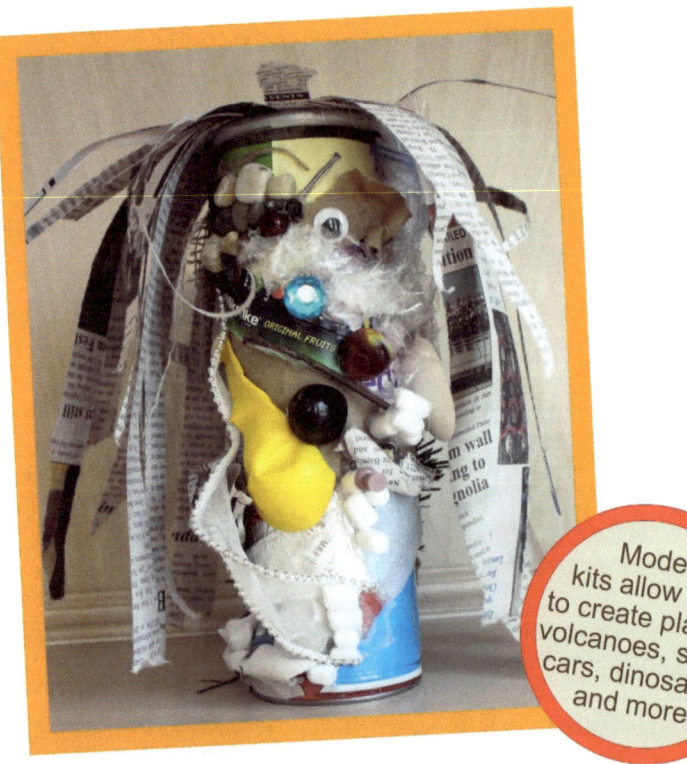

Model kits allow you to create planes, volcanoes, ships, cars, dinosaurs, and more!

This junk sculpture was made from a Pringles can, ribbon, newspaper, a balloon, rocks, gems, a googly eye, burlap, paper, foam, chip wrappers, Styrofoam, garland, nails, candy boxes, plastic ware, and a plastic bag. The can still opens and is now a great hiding spot for valuables.

1/2 N' 1/2

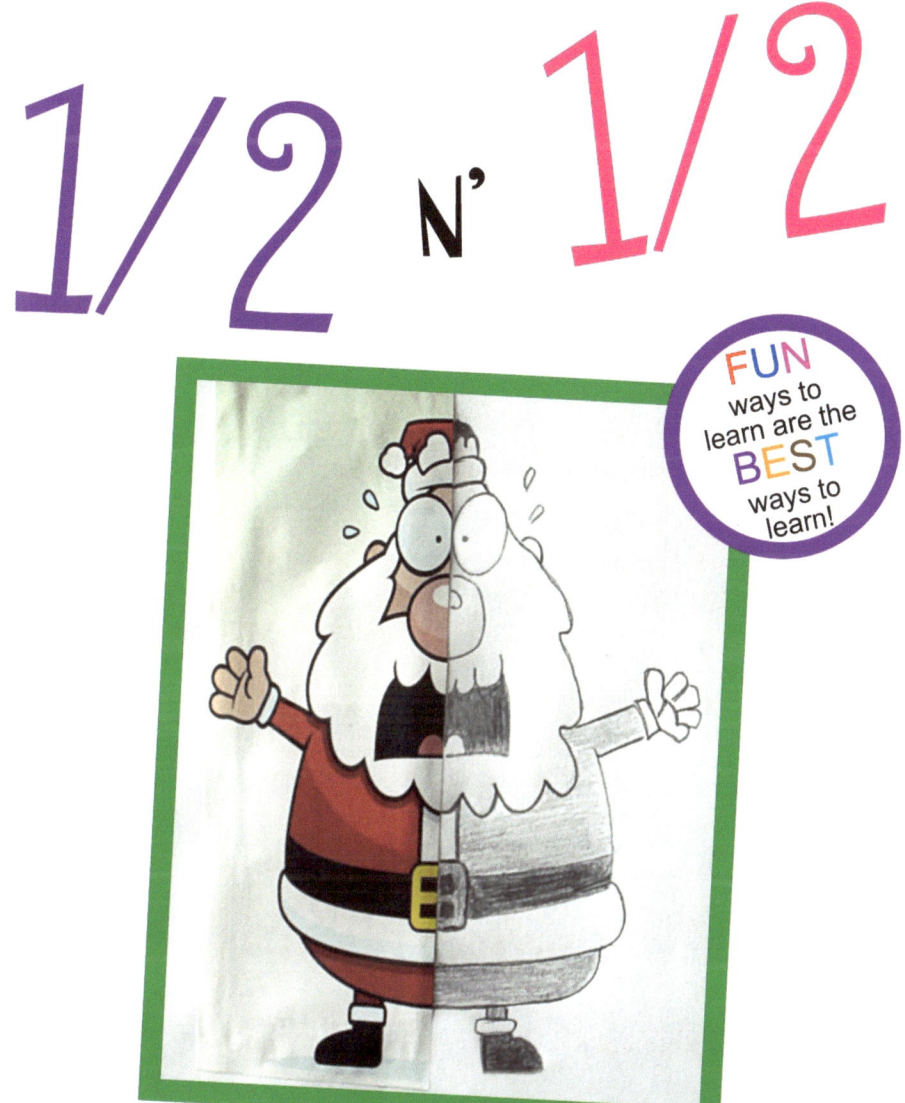

Draw the picture symmetrically, asymmetrically, realistically, or abstractly. Select a lined graphic or challenge yourself by choosing a photo.

Step 1   Find a picture in a magazine
Step 2   Cut it in half
Step 3   Paste one half to a piece of paper
Step 4   Complete the other half of the picture

Draw 3D

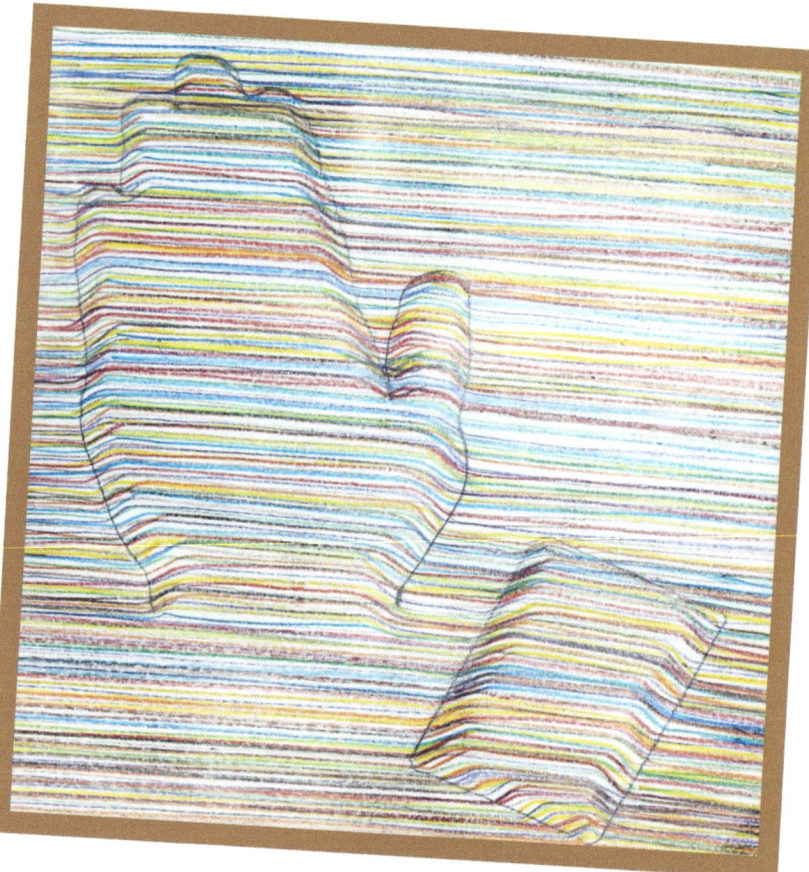

Lines can be one or more colors and it's okay if they are a bit crooked or overlap. The higher the bump, the more raised the object will look.

Step 1   Outline an object with a black line

Step 2   Draw straight lines across the page

Step 3   Bump the lines up as you reach the object

Step 4   Bump the lines down as you pass the object

PHOTO *Letters*

Step 1   Look for letters in everyday items

Step 2   Zoom in on the letters and take pictures

Step 3   Print the pictures

Step 4   Frame each letter or paste them together

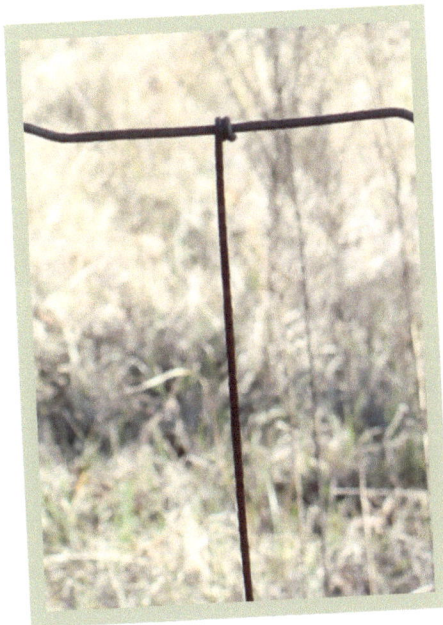
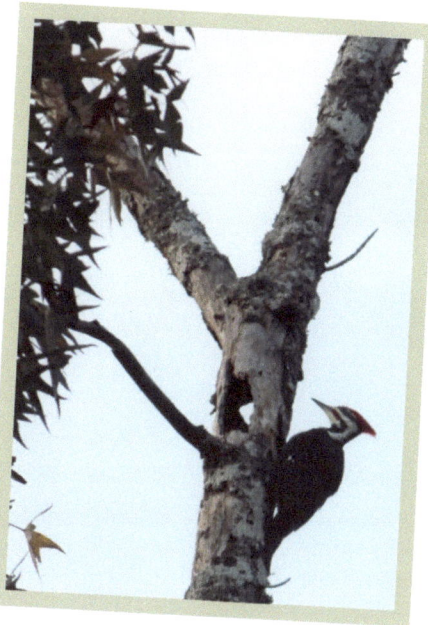

Take pictures or look for hidden letters in old photographs or magazine illustrations. Paste the photos together or frame them individually to form names and words. Look for high contrast between the letter and the background so the letter pops!